Mother Me and Mantel

In this autobiography some names, places and details have been changed to protect the privacy of individuals.

Cover Shutterstock photo by LedyX
Cover design by Sue Harrison

Chapter 1

Mother

This book has been in the back of my mind for a long time. Eventually, I felt urged to tackle it and the word tackle describes perfectly the task I set myself. I was under no illusion that the experience of writing this book would be difficult and in parts painful ... it was.

I'm just an ordinary person. Nevertheless, writing and sharing my story is something I felt I had to do. By no stretch of the imagination did I experience a happy and stable childhood. On the other hand, it was not as bad as some are forced to go through.

I suppose, if I am honest, I've written this for myself, a diary of my life if you like and it has been a cathartic experience. I hope my story will encourage others who may happen to read it.

So much of the initial part of the story was buried deep in my mind. Trying to bring those memories to the surface and
present them in a coherent way and in some sort of chronological order has been challenging. Later parts of my story were easier, as I had diaries to refer to.

With my hand on my heart, I can honestly say that what I've chosen to share in the pages of this book, are true to my memory of them. Some people's names have been changed to protect their identity.

It would be nice to think that my story might help someone and encourage them to share their story. I believe every person has a book inside them ... a story to tell, a testimony to share. I would like to think my book might be the encouragement they need to put pen to paper.

** **

I've realised while writing this, that my story is as much about my mother's life as my own. Much of what I've written comes from the things she told me, as I was too young to know. Most was shared when I was much older, when our fractured relationship was healed. In some ways I wish I had asked her more about that time ... about her life.

For me, so much of my early life is like a jigsaw with numerous pieces missing. I can only relate to what I can remember as seen and experienced through the eyes of a traumatised child. There are many forms of abuse. In my later years, I realised the abuse I suffered was emotional ... in its own way crippling.

My mother Irene was born in Hammersmith London on the 16th of July 1924. As a young girl she suffered with St Vitus dance a severe neurological disorder which meant she spent the majority of her early years in hospital. The experience affected her badly, she feared anyone in positions of authority, especially women. This was due in part to the unsympathetic treatment she received while she was there. Most of her schooling took place in the hospital. Unable to mix with other children she became shy and reclusive.

However, once she recovered, life became more normal for her, although the memories remained with her for many years, effecting how she related to people. I understand from what she told me, some of the nurses lacked the kindness and compassion a sick child needed.

As a young woman she worked in Dorothy Perkins, on Oxford Street, a job she said she loved. She told me about a Jewish lady who worked in the shop with her. Hearing about the political upheaval in Germany and the gradual rise of anti-Semitism, the woman was in a constant state of terror. She feared if war broke out, the Germans would invade England. As a Jewish woman she feared for her life. Mother said she felt so sorry for the woman and often thought about her.

With the eventual outbreak of the Second World War, mother and the family moved to Swindon, where I believe my grandfather worked for the railway. After the war, he worked in a factory.

With men away at war, women were needed to do their work. Mother took a job in a munitions factory, but unable to cope with the noise, she left and joined the land army, working on a large estate in the Wiltshire countryside.

She enjoyed the life and told me her two favourite things was driving the rickety old milk van, and singing with the band at the US military base, which was situated not far from where she was living. I remember she had a good voice.

She told me when she finished singing. She would make her way back to the farm in the early hours of the morning and with no sleep she would help load the van and then drive around the area delivering the milk. The things we get up to when we are young. But from what she said, even with a war going on. I believe it was a happy time for her.

After the war, she returned home to her parents in Swindon. I'm not sure where she worked, but I know she met a man … a man she cared deeply for. However, with no real explanation he ended their relationship and disappeared out of her life and that's when she met my father James. Going into a relationship on the rebound is never a good idea.

However, she fell for my father, a charming and good looking man. He was an accomplished artist and also an excellent dancer. Mother loved to dance. But he was not a nice man. He was out to get her, not because he had any love for her, but because he disliked the family. He called her mother [my grandmother] her ladyship. He considered the whole family to be snobs.

His own mother had a bad reputation. He was the youngest of three brothers, all of whom had different absentee fathers. I later learned from my mother, that my father was a bitter and angry man. Due in part she believed to his desire to go to Art College. But his mother was in no position to send him, even if she wanted to, which she didn't. She mocked him, apparently saying things like, 'We want no poncy artist in this family. You go to work with your brothers in the factory.' He had no option but to go and he hated it.

Loving art myself, I can imagine how much this hurt him. In many ways it must have destroyed him. In my later years, knowing this softened my attitude towards him. I could understand how he felt. How frustrated he must have been and unfulfilled. For someone with an artistic nature it would have been soul destroying.

To make matters worse, my mother's father [my grandfather] worked in the same factory. He was a supervisor and high up in the union, which added to my father's dislike of mother's family. And I think in his jealousy he determined to ruin my mother. He knew my grandmother disliked him. In fact she disliked the whole family.

My mother wept when she told me how on her wedding day. My grandmother fell to her knees, clutched at mother's wedding dress and begged her not to marry my father. "He will drag you into the gutter," she said. These were words mother never forgot.

As time went on she was forced to admit, her mother was right. But my mother was desperate to be a bride and have a family. She adored babies and was eager to have one of her own. She ignored her mother's warning and went ahead anyway, even though in her heart she knew it was wrong.

She admitted to me, with the cost of the wedding and all the preparation, she felt afraid to cancel it. Even though grandmother insisted it was not a problem. Marrying the wrong man was the problem. I can't imagine the tension on that day. Hardly joyful, when you know your family are not happy about your choice of husband.

After they were married, my parents moved to Lydiard Park, near Swindon. It was just after the war and due to the obvious shortage of available homes. People were being housed in huts once used by the military. They were supposed to be temporary accommodation. Temporary being the operative word, as they were still being used as homes in the sixties.

Not long after that, in 1947 I was born. Mother said the homes were pretty basic. But after the war and with little money, it was all they could afford. She told me, the year of my birth was the coldest winter on record with snow above the doors of the houses. This was followed by a blistering summer. She found it hard, as in July the summer heat reached its peak and she was pregnant with me.

Life was hard as they were short of money. My grandparents helped her to acquire everything necessary for a new baby, including a pram and a cot.

I arrived on July 7th after a long and painful birth. My mother said it was awful, hours past and one of the nurses grew impatient. She said the nurse slapped her and told her not to make such a fuss. Her words were, "I bet you didn't make this fuss when you conceived it." Hearing that, I was horrified! I was her first child and understandably she was scared. It seems they were like that in those days.

I weighed five pounds at birth and mother said I was too weak to breast feed and she ended up with Mastitis. She always insisted that was the cause. The nurses bound her tight with bandages and I was fed with a bottle. Unfortunately, I couldn't take the milk and began losing weight. My grandmother suggested it might help if mother diluted the milk. It worked. I thrived and soon gained weight. But feeding me was only the beginning of the problems.

It turned out my father had a serious gambling addiction. Everything my mother had bought, or been given for me, he took and used to pay his gambling depts. She was forced to walk out of the hospital with me and nothing else. The pram and cot bought by my grandparents, he sold.

Added to that, at birth my head was covered with a down of fiery red hair. Mother hated it. My father had bright auburn hair and my resemblance to the man she was beginning to dislike, was a slap in the face. Not only that, they rowed about his gambling and the fact he had taken all the new baby things to sell. His response was to tell her, she could shove me back where I came from. When she told me, I was shocked and hurt. It felt as though my own father cursed me.

I can't tell you how I felt. My mother said, even though she was struggling to bond with me, his cruel words upset her. I suppose you could say all these different events were the nail in our relationship coffin.

She had always wanted babies and even though she found herself in an unhappy marriage, she was thrilled when she found out she was pregnant. But from the time of my birth it all went wrong. The colour of my hair was the last straw.

My grandmother tried to convince her, the red hair would fall out ... which it did. Nevertheless, my mother rejected me. That's not to say I was neglected, she did her best. I imagine under difficult circumstances. But in my younger years when I needed her most, she wasn't there for me.

It seems we lived in Lydiard Park for a few years, in what I understand were difficult circumstances. My father's gambling increased, so much so, the people he owed money to, would wait for him outside the factory gates and take all his wages. Mother told me she was seldom given any money and in those days there was no such thing as child support.

By this time, mother had two more children, my brother Edward and our much younger sister Margaret. With three children to look after, she was unable to go out to work. She did her best to keep us clothed and fed, while having little to eat herself.

My grandmother would bring us food and make clothes for us, and a kind butcher who also lived in the park would give my mother occasional meat without charge. Unfortunately, when father came home from work, he would find the food and eat it. It didn't matter where she hid it, he always found it.

On numerous occasions, mother would leave and take us to her parents. They would let us stay for a while, but eventually insist she go back home to my father. Their sympathy was muted as mother had married against their wishes. My grandmother would say, 'You have made your bed. Now you must lie in it.'

Each time mother returned, she said my father would force himself on her, never letting her rest until he had his way.

With three young children to look after, starved of food and basically raped most nights. Life must have been hell for her. However, help came in a most unexpected way.

Over time mother became poorly. Thin and weak she went to the doctor and was diagnosed with severe malnutrition. Frequent visits were made to the doctor and overtime it would seem their relationship changed from doctor and patient, to being lovers.

I know my mother's life revolved around this man. He was sixteen years older than her, but she was besotted and looked upon him as her saviour. She was blind to anything or anyone else, including us children … as was he. We were an appendage around their necks. To mother, we were a constant reminder of the trauma she had suffered while living with my father.

My understanding of the situation at this time is vague, due to my young age. From what my mother told me, Doctor Rodman took us away from my father and hid us in a caravan. I have no idea in what part of the country it was. Probably somewhere in Wiltshire

It must have been a hard time for my mother and the Doctor. They needed to keep their relationship secret. Not easy to keep a low profile, when you have three children cooped up in a small caravan, with other people around taking note of the situation.

Two instances spring to mind that could have caused a lot of trouble for them. I'm not sure where my mother and Doctor Rodman were. But my young brother somehow got hold of a jar of caustic oven cleaner. He managed to open the jar and eat some of the contents. I can still remember his screams and mothers panic as the Doctor rushed them to the local hospital.

I imagine we all had to go, as there was no one to take care of us on the caravan site. Fortunately, he survived, but from what mother told me years later it was a close call. It was fortunate that it was the weekend and the Doctor was with us. Mother could drive, but at the time she didn't have a car.

Another incident involved me. I must have been playing outside the van and wondered into the woods which were close by. I was playing when a man appeared. To me as a small five or six year old he seemed huge. I remember he held out some sweets. I don't remember his exact words, but it was on the lines of, "Come with me little girl, and I'll give you a sweet."

Fortunately, mother called me. I could see her standing on the steps of the caravan. My words to him I do remember, "I have to go," I said. "My mummy is calling me." Oblivious of the danger I'd been in, I turned and ran to her. I don't know if she had seen the man I was talking to. But I remember she was extremely cross with me.

One of my more pleasant memories, were nights in the caravan. If my brother and I went to bed without a fuss, mother would let us listen to the Archers. I loved lying in my bunk smelling the gas lamps and listening to the radio. When the Archers finished she would turn our lamps off and close the partition door. Before falling asleep I would listen to the muted radio and mother moving around. Even now, if I'm in an old caravan, I still like the smell when the gas lamps are lit. It evokes memories which at that time weren't all bad.

Nevertheless, it was strange time. I didn't understand what was happening. In some ways even now when I reflect on it, it doesn't seem real. But it's a memory that remains with me. I don't know how long we lived in the caravan. Mother didn't say much about it. I think it was a time she chose to forget.

retired from teaching, but occasionally took on troublesome children like me. She was a large lady. Dressed in her black habit, her presence filled the small room. She may have been attractive when she was younger, but in old age she had acquired lumps on her face and long whiskers. Which I admit I found fascinating.

But no matter how she looked, she of all the nuns in that school got the best out of me. When I left, I could spell quite well. She is one of the many women that over the years had a positive influence on my life.

I didn't know God and yet as I reflect on my younger years, it was as if He provided mother figures for me. Even as a young working woman, there were women friends who influenced me. Dare I say brought out the best in me, and in those days that was quite a feat, as I was pretty mixed up.

While at school, my teachers and parents felt something was wrong with me. Something was wrong. I was unloved, unhappy and insecure. My parents decided I should see a psychiatrist. They were oblivious to the fact, that if I'd had their love and acceptance, I would have been a different child. No doubt with a different future. I suppose the same could be said for my brother. However, I now know every situation we face in life is in God's plan.

I remember sitting in the psychiatrist's office not saying much. She saw me on a number of occasions and during one of the sessions, she organised an official IQ test. Much to my parent's amazement, I passed with flying colours. The psychiatrist, having spent time talking to me challenged my parents about my home life situation. She told them as I was nearly fourteen, I should have more freedom and pocket money.

Her intervention caused even more trouble for me. My mother was furious that the psychiatrist appeared to be blaming them for what mother called my defiant and rebellious behaviour. Nevertheless, my parents gave me some pocket money and a little more freedom, in as much as I was allowed to go to bed later than my brother and sister.

Overtime, we were encouraged to look upon Doctor Rodman as our father, and to call him daddy. Having not known our real father, this became natural. Life was hard, not in a deprived way, but in the way we were brought up, in the lack of attention and love.

Doctor Rodman's upbringing had been strict … Victorian. Children were to be seen and not heard. He spent most of his young life in a boy's boarding school in Lancashire. He lived a regimented life at home and at school. Nevertheless, he excelled and chose a career as a Doctor.

However, he brought his strict loveless

upbringing into his life with our mother. In the kitchen he hung up a cane painted yellow and black. Put there to remind us what would happen should we misbehave. (No wonder I hate wasps so much.) My brother was the most regular recipient of this discipline.

We had a housekeeper, Mrs Randel, a lovely lady. She had the unfortunate job of taking care of us when we came home from school. Our parents would be downstairs in the surgery, mother worked as father's receptionist.

Mrs Randel would fix our meals and make sure we did our homework. Our meals were basic. We were not allowed luxuries like butter, we had Stork margarine. We were allowed sweets on a Sunday, but only if we had been good.

We were not allowed in the lounge, unless invited, or were being introduced to someone. Much was made of my sister at these times. But as for me and Edward, it was dismissive. I always remember my introduction at these times … not complimentary. My stepfather would say, "This is our eldest. We are not expecting her to amount to much."

In my own defence, as I've said before, at the age of five I read well. Books enabled me to escape the disturbing life going on around me. My favourites were Enid Blyton's books, especially 'The far Away Tree,' and 'The Secret Seven.'

One of the rare things I enjoyed at school was when the teacher read to us. I always looked forward to that time.

Edward couldn't read. I don't think he ever did. When I think about him, it could be that he was severely dyslexic. In those days … in the fifties, such a thing was not really known about. I now know I am mathematically dyslexic. Both of us were a cause of great frustration to our parents. Even with all the disturbance and insecurity in our young lives, they had little or no understanding and certainly no sympathy. They were so wrapped up in each other, we were of no importance. We were to be seen and not heard.

The only person who showed us kindness was Mrs Randel. In fact she taught me how to tell the time. My mathematics was so bad, at the age of twelve I still couldn't tell the time. She promised, if I would learn to tell the time within a week, she would buy me a watch. With her patient teaching I did. She bought me a Timex. Such a pretty watch, I loved it.

However, one afternoon before I was able to tell the time and had the watch. I asked mother if I could ride my bike to Mrs Godsland's house. She lived close by and was the lady we stayed with when our parents went on holiday. Margaret wanted to come with me. Mother told us to be careful and to get home at six o'clock, as we were having fish and chips … a real treat, we were excited.

We were enjoying ourselves so much, I lost track of time. Worried it must be getting late. I asked somebody the time. When they said it was nearly seven o'clock I panicked. I knew I would be in big trouble. Urging my little sister to ride fast, we raced home.

Our reception was cold in the extreme. We were dragged up to our room. (My sister and I shared a room with bunk beds.) We were denied food and left to think about our lack of responsibility. Margaret curled on her bed crying. I lay on the top bunk, my stomach churning, half from hunger and half nerves. Apart from the occasional use of the wasp stick, mothers other favourite punishment tool was the icy silent treatment. Something I received regularly.

Hearing footsteps approaching, we both sat up. Mother came in and took Margaret's hand. Glaring at me she snapped, "You can stay here and think about what you did." There were no words to express the pain in my heart as I watched her take Margaret out of the room. I knew my sister would be forgiven and have something to eat.

I think it was probably one of the worst times in my life, and there have been many. My step father had no time for me. But knowing my own mother who I adored, really didn't like me. The feeling of rejection was more painful than I could express. I lay there and sobbed. As a youngster, I didn't know God, but I cried out to Him. "Why was I born? I didn't ask to be born."

I remember many times on my own in the

room. I would stare into the mirror and ask, "Who am I?" I didn't know who I was asking, God, I suppose. All through my childhood and early years, I remember the fear and debilitating sense of insecurity. I wasn't loved or wanted.

I wasn't physically abused, but I was emotionally. I would have to say the same for my brother. But even though my parents made it obvious that only Margaret mattered. I still loved my little sister. She was my constant shadow, but I didn't mind.

I was crazy about horses and in the summer months, I would ride my bike for miles looking for a farm that had a pony I could ride. I would help the farmer in exchange for a ride. My goodness, you wouldn't do that these days!

I was a strange mixture, shy and retiring, while at the same time strong and confident. I thank God the strong and confident surfaced in my later years.

Due to our lack of relationship and my insecurity, my parents only saw the shy me. The child with a huge inferiority complex … under the circumstances it was hardly surprising. The fact they thought me stupid was drilled into me from an early age. I carried this inferiority into adulthood.

I remember one time, my sister and I wanted to dance for them. I was probably about eleven, my sister would have been around five or six years old. It was one of the rare times we were allowed in the sitting room. My stepfather put on his recording of Swan Lake for us and Margaret and I danced together. We twirled around doing our best to be ballerinas.

My sister was a pretty little blond girl. Me on the other hand, I was at that podgy awkward stage. I'll always remember their laughter and comments. "My goodness, you look like an elephant clomping around." It wasn't said as an endearing joke. It was meant to be cruel, and I took it as such. I never did anything like that again.

Whenever I was in trouble, my mother would shout, "Look at me!" I never could make eye contact with either of them. All part of the inferiority complex I suppose. But then why would I want to look into the eyes of someone who disliked me?

I wanted to make them proud of me. To disprove their words, 'She will not amount to much.'

Sadly, I had a habit of making matters worse. For example, one day after school, while dressed in my uniform, I was seen by one of my father's patients riding on a local rag and bone man's cart. Unbeknown to mother, I used to ride my bike to his yard and he would let me ride the pony. I must admit I took some risks. Mother quickly put a stop to it.

However, when they were told about me riding on the cart, things turned nasty. When I got home, the wasp cane appeared and I knew I was in real trouble. Beside herself, mother raged at me. "I've told you before. Your father is a Doctor, well known in this town. You have a responsibility to behave properly." My father just sat in the chair watching. Thinking about it, I now realise he was most likely drunk, which would have added to my mother's anger. At the time being young, I had no idea he had a drink problem.

She made to punish me with the cane, but I'm afraid all the anger and hurt inside me rose to the surface. There was no love between us. I felt she meant to humiliate me. It wasn't my safety she cared about, it was their reputation. I had humiliated them and sullied my stepfather's position in the town.

We fought physically and I fled the room. I'm not sure how old I was, maybe thirteen. I ran away and must have walked miles, it felt like it. It was getting dark, so I sheltered in a covered bus stop and sat on the seat.

At first I didn't notice the police station across the road. Not until a policeman walked across to me. Afraid I was going to be arrested I remained quiet. I didn't know if my parents had rung the police. He convinced me to accompany him into the police station. When they gave me a cup of tea, I relaxed and told them my name.

Having given them my address, they were able to contact my parents. Mother didn't want me home, and I didn't want to go. So the police rang the number she gave them. It was a friend of my step father, Doctor Jaff. He picked me up from the police station and I stayed with him and his housekeeper for about a week. I enjoyed my time with him and didn't want to go home.

During this time I found out about my father's alcoholism. Doctor Jaff, a recovering alcoholic was my father's support. Both of them were in AA. I was too young to fully understand the situation, but it answered a few questions. For example, when we were little, we would be picked up in the middle of the night by my uncle and aunty May and driven to their house in Kent, where we remained for a few days, sometimes longer. One time, we stayed with my aunt for an extended period and I went with my cousin to her school. I can't say I enjoyed it much. It was a time of confusion and upheaval.

The whole situation heightened my sense of insecurity. I missed mother and had bad dreams. My Aunt did her best to comfort me. Now, when I reflect on it, it must have been hard for them, trying to cope with three traumatised children. This happened a few times, some for longer spells than others.

Many years later mother told me, my step father was never violent when drunk. He became maudlin and as she put it, pathetic. She had the responsibility of sobering him up and trying to hide his drunkenness from the patients. He would hide bottles of whisky all over the house and even in his desk in the surgery. It must have been a nightmare for her. Doctor Jaff would always come to assist her.

From what she told me, my father had no idea he was an alcoholic. His wife drove him to it. To

27

drown his sorrows, one day he went to their local pub and too late he realised he had a problem. Other people could drink without ill affect, but for him it was like poison. That first drink pushed him down a slippery slope. Of course his wife latched onto it and made his life a misery.

Eventually, my mother and step father had a huge row. I do remember my mother screaming and shouting, before my uncle drove us to his house in Kent. Mother said she threatened to leave him, if he didn't stop drinking and she meant it. Her ultimatum drove him to AA, where he was partnered with Doctor Jaff.

With Jaffs help, support from AA, and mothers love, he had the courage to confess his problem and begin to overcome it. In later years I remember him talking about that time. How much he appreciated Doctor Jaff and A A. He always said that for him, the higher power spoken of in AA was God.

A quiet Christian, my step father enjoyed going to church. Mother told me in the mornings at home, he would read his bible and pray. He would try to encourage my mother to pray, but she didn't understand.

Mother told me how he would ask God to make a way for them to marry. A number of years later, his prayers were answered. His estranged wife moved back to South Africa where she died, enabling them to get married. He always insisted it was a miracle, as she never once made it public that he was living with another woman, which in those days would have ruined him. I suppose she thought not divorcing him increased her power over him. My step father would always insist, his ex-wife's silence about his relationship with mother was divine protection, mother agreed and so do I.

A few years later they did marry. I had left home by then. They married in secret. The only people to attend were my Aunt and Uncle and my mother's parents. No patients ever found out. Absolutely no one in the town new, even we children were unaware of their marriage. We were told a few months later. After marrying, they shared an idyllic life together.

Chapter 3

ME

After spending a pleasant week with Doctor Jaff, I was forced to go home. I was greeted with a hostile silence. It was a painful and traumatic time. The atmosphere in the house when I returned was unbearable. I really think at that time my mother had gone from disliking me to outright hate. I have to confess, I felt much the same about her. As a thirteen year old, my emotions were all over the place. I hated her, but at the same time I loved her desperately. To be honest you could have cut the atmosphere with a knife. Most of that time is a blank. Obviously, I continued going to school.

In my younger days, things just seemed to happen. But I suppose when you are young other people like parents organise your life and you have little say in the matter. For example, one day my mother informed me, I was leaving home and going to work in a kennels. I was nearly fifteen and still at school. I remember just staring at her. I knew she wanted rid of me.

In less than a week she had taken me shopping to buy the work clothes recommended by the lady I was to work for. They were brown coloured overalls and wellington boots. Naively, I had little understanding of what was going on. In a way, to me it was an adventure. My emotions bounced between excitement and anxiety.

Because my school was private, it enabled my parents to take me away before my fifteenth birthday. In a way I felt excited, pleased to be leaving school, which I hated. The nuns were not nice. Apart from the one I had grown fond of. She is someone I have never forgotten.

On the day mother drove me to the kennels, my initial excitement turned to anxiety. We travelled in a tense silence. I remember the unpleasant atmosphere in the car. The journey seemed endless, although it wasn't far from home. When we arrived at the kennels, mother introduced me to the owners and left. I remember how I felt as I watched her drive away. Heartbroken was an understatement. I felt abandoned, rejected and scared.

The couple I was to work for were strange and unfriendly. I guess my parents had told them I was difficult, because the tall thin woman stared at me, her expression hard and unfriendly as she reeled off a list of does and don'ts.

I was introduced to two other girls, they were older than me, but both of them were nice. I quickly realised the younger girl was our employers favourite, she was told to show me to my room. It was basic but comfortable.

I had a small bed, a dressing table and a wardrobe, not that I had many clothes. The house itself was more of a large bungalow. But as to décor or anything else of interest, I really can't remember. Over time I chose to blank out a lot of the memories. Most of which were distressing.

It was a noisy place. I felt sure the dogs incessant barking would drive me mad. Even at night they barked, especially those boarding while their owners were on holiday. I felt I would never get used to the noise, but surprisingly, after a while I did.

It wasn't a big place. Most of the kennels were built on the top of a grassy bank. The rest were lower down, along with the grooming parlour and food shed. Apart from boarding people's dogs and cats, the owners of the place also bred and showed Dalmatians, Boxers and wire haired terriers.

I know if people had realised how the place was run they would never have brought their animals there. It was awful. I hated it and had never felt so unhappy.

The food wasn't good either and there was never enough of it. I was always hungry. Sometimes we had bacon for breakfast. Nice you might think, but in reality it was going off and looked a strange colour. I didn't eat it. Driven by hunger, when no one was looking I would eat the dog's biscuits. They were bone shaped and tasteless but they filled a hole. I had to be careful as these were for their show dogs and the amount was limited.

Each morning we had to be up and working by seven o'clock. Each dog, especially boarders had to be taken for a walk. The kennels was built on a busy road, but we walked the dogs two at a time along the wide grass verge.

Whenever a bus passed me on its way to my home town, the feeling of loss and abandonment was overwhelming. Strangely, it felt as though the busses were my mother. I know that sounds crazy. I've since realised they simply represented my loss and need for her ... my desire to be home. Even though I knew she didn't want me, I still loved and needed her.

Living and working at the kennels was torture. We worked all hours and in all weathers. The food was basic and limited. I was fifteen and always hungry.

For me, the most traumatic experience was when people brought in their male cats to be neutered and their dogs to be put down. I'm pretty sure the owners had no idea of the cruelty their pets suffered. If they had I'm sure they would have reported it. I can't imagine their cats were ever the same after their traumatic experience.

Everything unpleasant was done by the husband. The poor cats had their heads and front feet forced into a sack. We had the awful job of helping him with this. He wore gloves, we had nothing to protect our hands as the poor cats fought and screamed. Once the cat was secured, he used a scalpel to do the job. It makes me feel ill, just talking about it.

The cruelty of the people I was forced to work for was beyond my understanding. The cat's owners payed a high price for this service, and I don't mean in money. After such an experience, I can't imagine the poor traumatised animals were ever the same again.

People also brought their white boxers in to be destroyed. They are known to be blind or deaf ... in some cases both. These were grown dogs, but not old or ailing. Why have a white boxer, if you're going to let it grow up and then have it put down. These people probably knew a vet might not be willing, and if they were, the price even in the early sixties would be high. So they brought the poor animals to our kennels.

Once the owner left, we would leave the dogs in a kennel for an hour or two and then take it round the back of the food shed where there was an old tree with a metal ring fixed in the trunk.

For quite a while I had nothing to do with what went on round there. However, one day at breakfast I was told a dog was being brought in and it would be me helping him with it.

To say I was horrified and scared was an understatement. When the time came, I had to fetch the poor animal and bring it to the tree. I remember it was a friendly dog. The boss told me to thread the rope through the metal ring, pull the dog close to the tree trunk and wind the rest around the tree. I was then told to hold on tight and look away.

The poor dog struggled and cried. I shouldn't have watched, but I did. I don't know what I imagined was going to happen. As a naive young person I thought he was going to inject the dog. But having been told to look away, I should have known better. I had been in this place long enough to know how things worked.

Horrified, I watched the man take a gun out of a case on the ground. Too late, I realised what he was going to do. I started to cry and my grip on the rope loosened. He yelled at me. The dog was choking and struggling. I was terrified of loud bangs and guns. This experience increased that fear a hundred fold.

He told me to pull the rope tight. The dog uttered a strangled cry as he put the barrel under its left ear. My heart was pounding, tears streamed down my face. He was still shouting at me. Terrified and panic stricken, I accidently released the rope slightly, but enough that when he fired the gun the dog moved and was hit in the top of its head instead of under the ear.

The air was blue with the man's language. The poor dog was screaming and struggling. I stood in a state of shock. Hearing the animals distress and realising it was suffering brought me too my senses. I pulled on the rope and the man killed the dog.

As you can tell this is an experience I have never and will never forget. I remember every detail. I can see it in my mind. It haunts me. Especially as I still feel so many years later that I caused that poor animals suffering.

One good thing that came out of that experience, I was never told to do it again. I didn't even have to help in the drowning of any white puppies born to the kennels own boxer dogs. Unfortunately, boxers can give birth to as many as twelve pups. Sadly, sometimes more than half of a litter can be born white.

They would remove them and drown them in a barrel of water. It was heart breaking to witness. The poor little things would struggle for life. Once they were dead, they were thrown on a huge fire round the back of the buildings along with dead adult dogs and anything else that needed burning.

The smell when it was lit was revolting. It was hard to get the smell out of my nose. This place played a huge part in the hardening of my heart.

Everything that went on seemed to feed the anger, and rejection I felt inside.

I believe I was a gentle and sensitive child. Had I experienced a loving family life, I'm sure I would have grown to be a different person. But we are what life makes us. Perhaps in some way, all my experiences good and bad helped me to be the survivor I became later in life.

Chapter 4

I spent a miserable year in the kennels. The thought of staying there much longer was unbearable. However, as a young fifteen year old, I had no idea what to do or where to go. I knew my mother wouldn't have me home. The couple who owned the kennels were not happy with me, any more than I was with them. So my options were limited.

My life at the kennels had been awful. Their treatment of animals was beyond anything I could understand. The horror of the place would stay with me for ever. I'll be honest, as a naive fifteen year old all I wanted was to go home, be loved by my mother and have my own pony. Nice dream.

One day, I received something I'd never had, a letter. Instantly I thought it was from my mother, telling me I could come home. I remember my excitement as with trembling hands I tore the envelope open. Pulling out the two page letter, I anticipated reading my mother's words. However, it wasn't from mother.

At first I had no idea who it was from, until I read these lines, I remember them well. 'Your mother has contacted me to say that having coped with you all these years. It is now my turn to look after you, as she does not wish you to go back to them.'

The letter was from my birth father. He went on to say he would be coming to London and I should get a train to Victoria station and he would meet me there. Enclosed in the letter was money for a ticket.

As I reread the letter, I had mixed emotions. I was excited at the thought of a new adventure, but realising my mother was washing her hands of me, left me with a deep sense of loss. I cried a lot and kept myself to myself. I had to show the letter to my employers as I needed the day off.

When the day came and I caught the bus to our local station, I was almost breathless with anticipation. On arrival at Victoria I was filled with excitement. I don't remember if arrangements had been made with regard to recognising each other, suffice to say we did. He had a young girl with him, it was his stepdaughter. She was a bit older than me.

Once the rather awkward introductions were made, my father took us to the station café for a drink. The rest of the day we spent at London Zoo. Loving animals, I enjoyed it.

At lunch time he asked me how I felt about going to live with him and his knew family. I was young, frightened and insecure. I had no relationship or feelings for this man. He was my father in name only. He had rejected me, as he had my siblings.

In my life, his was the first of many rejections. The pain went deep. It could have defined me, but I managed through my life to hide the pain and use it as a defence against any kind of closeness, especially with men. As I got older, I quickly learned to manipulate them.

However, I digress. Before we left the zoo he bought us both a present in the gift shop. Of all the things I could have chosen, why a large china tiger? Maybe subconsciously, I was trying to say something. I hung onto it for a few years, but eventually it got broken.

After meeting and spending time with him, it was decided I would leave the kennels and go to Swindon and live with him and his new family. It had been an emotionally exhausting day. There had been so much to discuss, a decision had to be made and it was down to me to make it.

Even as a young person, I knew I had little choice. No way could I remain a day longer in the kennels and I couldn't go home. So I chose the only option available to me, a new life with my father and his family, in the town where I was born.

My mind buzzed with excitement and anxious thoughts as I made my way back to the kennels. I had to give at least a week's notice before I could leave. I remember it being the worst week of my life, it dragged interminably. Even though I felt anxious about living with my father, I also looked upon it as an adventure.

Questions rolled round in my head. Where did they live? Would I get on with his wife and daughter? The daughter seemed nice enough, but we had only spent a day together. As a young teenager, it didn't occur to me to think about his wife, or how she might be feeling at the prospect of having her husband's estranged daughter in her home. I was nervous about meeting her. I imagine she felt the same about meeting me.

I was so happy when the day came to leave the kennels. Standing on the road outside the place, I breathed a sigh of relief as I waited for the bus. Working in the kennels had been nothing but hardship and unhappiness. Clutching my small suitcase, I tried to imagine what life would be like from now on.

My father had given me money for the journey and was meeting me in London. We would travel together to Swindon. I knew moving to Swindon meant I would be further away from my mother, and such as it was, my family. Mixed with my excitement were feelings of confusion, hurt and a deep sense of insecurity.

*****

I felt anxious when we arrived in Swindon. My father and his family lived in a council flat. I had to share a bedroom with their daughter. Even as a young person I was sensitive and quickly picked up on the tense atmosphere.

I don't remember my father's wife, but she was not unkind to me. Now as I write this so many years later, I can imagine how hard it must have been for her. I was a young teenager, with all that entails, and if you add to that all my buried hurt, she basically had a time bomb in her house.

I'm not naturally a hard person. However, my upbringing and life in general made me who I was. I admit I was wild and rebellious, filled with anger and a growing dislike of men. The only thing that gave me any enjoyment and made me smile was being around horses. I would ride whenever I could.

Anyway, back to living with my father and his family. To be honest, I don't remember much. Over the years I've realised I'm good at blanking things out of my mind, which unfortunately means I've forgotten a lot and the memories I have are fractured and sometimes out of sync.

You would think I would remember the time spent with my father. However, in many ways so much has happened in my life … so many different experiences, that I've acquired a selective memory. It's fascinating to talk to relatives and get their perspective on things. Many times they remember things I don't, and visa versa.

One time I do remember. I mentioned before what a good artist my father was. This particular day I sat beside him in the lounge and watched him draw a pretty vase. It was amazing, but it wasn't just the art work. For a brief time I felt close to him. We shared a love for something we were both good at … he was exceptional!

I've always been grateful that he passed the love of art and the ability to paint onto me. My mother's gift to me was a love of music and the ability to sing. So for those two abilities I am grateful to them. Although, I now know it is God who gives us our gifts and our talents.

I can't remember how long I lived with my father, probably not long. One day there was a heated argument involving my father, his wife and me. I don't remember what it was about, but I did what I was good at. I grabbed my bag, stormed out of the flat and ran to the bus stop. I don't know where I was going. It was fortunate that my father followed me, as I knew no one in Swindon. He tried to talk me into returning home with him. Me being me, I refused and when the bus arrived I got on it and so did he.

He talked me into going with him to his mother's house (my grandmother.) And then he had to talk her into letting me stay. I don't think I was there for long. Even in the early sixties, it was basic living. The facilities were outside, there was no toilet roll, just squares of newspaper tied together and fixed to a nail in the wall. At night it was a pot under the bed.

I remember what my mother had said about her ... she was known as a lady of the night. She was a large heavily corseted woman and not particularly friendly. She was quite brusque and mostly ignored me. I think she found the way I looked and what she called my posh accent, annoying. Basically, she couldn't wait to get rid of me.

I remember her as a hard woman, who liked to live life her way. As a young naive girl, I don't know if she was still working while I was with her. I didn't see or hear anything. But she must have made money to live somehow.

Anyway, I stayed with her for a while, but our relationship was a tense one. Then one day out of the blue a man and a woman arrived. It turned out this was my uncle Stan and his wife Ruby. I believe my Uncle was grandmother's eldest. I never met her third son.

My Aunt and Uncle were nice. I liked them, which was just as well, as my grandmother was palming me off on them. However, they didn't seem to mind. I was so relieved when they took me out to their car and drove me to their home. I was glad to be away from my grandmother. I only ever saw her once after that, many years later.

My Uncle lived in a nice street. Their house was a large semi, way nicer than my grandmother's grubby looking terraced property and my father's small council flat. I know, I'm sounding very snobbish.

They had two children, a boy quite a bit older than me and a young girl. I shared a room with the girl. Sadly, I can't remember their names ... selective memory again. Their son was an extremely good athlete, a runner if I remember rightly.

One particular day remains in my memory ... a happy day. I won a beauty contest at the factory where I was working and on that same day my cousin came home with a winner's trophy. My Aunt and Uncle were so proud of us both. We all went out for a celebratory meal.

Having someone be proud of me was a new and pleasant experience. I was happy while I was with them. I felt like I was accepted and part of the family. It was a disciplined but loving home.

However, my anger was never far from the surface. One day, my little cousin played with a small wooden chalet mother had brought for me from Switzerland. She brought two, one for me and one for my sister Margaret. They were music boxes and extremely pretty.

I loved this little wooden house. It was

especially precious as it was all I had of my mother. My cousin broke it. Sad to say, I went wild. I didn't actually hit my cousin, but I screamed in anger and finished off the small chalets destruction. I didn't want it anymore, she had broken it.

I remember my Aunt and Uncle ran upstairs. I can't recall what was said, but I remember my Aunt holding her daughter and my Uncle trying to calm me. They couldn't replace my broken Chalet, but they still continued to show me love. I believe they understood my distress.

I don't remember how long I lived with them, but eventually I wanted to go home. I missed my mother. Having made tentative contact with her by letter, I packed my few belongs said a tearful goodbye to my Uncle and the family and made my way back home.

My parents were now living in a spacious bungalow not far from town. Our reunion was a bit tense, but at the age of around seventeen, and benefiting from my Aunt and Uncles care, I had matured. The relationship was not close, but much improved.

I lived at home for nearly a year, working in a local factory making Garrard record players. My job was to solder bits of wire together. It was piece work, so you were payed according to how much work you did. Suffice to say I was useless at it, and I hated it. Whenever the union called us out on strike, I was one of the first out of the gate.

My whole life revolved around horses. If I heard the sound of hooves outside, I would rush to the window to look. My desire to work with them increased. I would purchase copies of Horse and Hound and scour the pages for work.

Eventually, I found an Equestrian centre looking for a stable hand, it was just outside Winchester. It sounded perfect so I went for an interview and got the job.

I know my mother and stepfather weren't bothered about me leaving. As for me, I was just excited to begin a job that had been a dream for so long. For me there was no longer any trauma involved with leaving … home sickness was now a thing of the past. I immersed myself in the life I had always wanted.

There were four of us stable girls; we shared a house on what was an extensive property. From what I can remember there were around twenty horses, most of which were stabled. Each of us girls had a set number of horses to care for. Across from the stables there was a spacious indoor school.

When I went for my interview I was introduced to the horses I might be looking after. There were five in all. One was a big black horse called Mace. He was an ex race horse. I still remember his name, probably because he was so scary. No one else wanted to look after him. I had a horrible feeling he would be among the five I was to look after. I was right.

On my first day of working there, I was shown to the stables and told that Mace was one of my five. That's what happens when you're the new girl on the block. You have to do what no one else wants to do. In this instance, it was to look after a big bad tempered horse. Strangely, I think if I had been there longer, he and I just might have become friends.

On my first day, I stood on the other side of his stable door and looked at him. With his ears back he glared at me. I admit, I was scared, but if I wanted to keep the job I was going to have to cope with him. Giving him his food was like taking your life in your hands. With his ears back and wild eyes, he would stretch out his neck and try to bite.

I resolved to be the boss and not allow him to bully and terrorize me. I would enter his stall with the food bucket and remain by the door until he obeyed my firm shout to move back. Trying to hide my nerves, I went to his trough and emptied the food into it, all the while keeping a wary eye on him and telling him to stay back. Fortunately he did.

Grooming him was fun. I had to stand on a stool to reach the top of his back. For my own safety I tied him up short, so that he couldn't reach round and bite me. The funny thing was, once you were riding him, he turned from being a devil to being an angel. Unless, when riding him at a canter, you made the mistake of leaning too far forward, in which case he reverted to being a race horse and took off at a gallop.

I had never been taught to ride. Compared to the others, it turned out I was pretty rough and ready. After a few lessons I did improve, but I was never going to be a great rider.

However, my ability to get the best out of young riders worked in my favour. I was given the job of teaching the little ones to ride. The parents liked the way I taught their children. Surprising really, as I can't say I like children that much.

But sadly, I was only there a short while and the place closed. The owners kindly found me employment in a small establishment that concentrated on breeding show ponies. They employed me not so much for my riding as for my handling skill.

In this place I shared a caravan on the yard with another girl. It was basic and not particularly comfortable. In the summer we sweltered, and in the winter we froze to death.

I remember returning from a ride. I dismounted and went to the caravan to find my working boots. As my frozen feet came back to life, I remember writhing on the bed, crying with pain.

It was hard work with long hours. Sometimes, if I was accompanying the ponies to a show, I would be up at five in the morning and wouldn't get to bed until late at night. But they were nice people and I enjoyed it. It was a healthy life and I was certainly fit.

I had never been a nervous rider. In fact some would say I was over confident. But having been bolted with on numerous occasions, I started to lose my nerve. Every morning before horse or rider had any breakfast, we would ride the young ponies out. Sometimes there would be as many as five of us riding down the lane in single file. It only took some noisy motorcyclist to ride past, and most of us would find ourselves in a hedge or galloping full pelt back to the stables.

Not much fun I can tell you. On reflection, we must have looked like the funny illustrations in the Norman Thelwell books. Some of us galloping wildly back to the stables, while others were extricating themselves from a hedge.

As each day past I became more nervous of riding. However, things changed for me the day my employer told me a sixteen hand hunter would be arriving, and I was to look after it. My heart fell. It was bad enough dealing with the naughty ponies. The thought of a huge powerful hunter just about freaked me out.

I will never forget my first introduction to Kerry Court. He arrived on my day off so I first saw him the next day. He was saddled and ready for me to ride out with the youngsters. I looked at him and my heart sank, *that's a long way to fall*, I thought.

My boss who was holding him smiled at me. She hoisted me into the saddle all the while reassuring me that the horse was a gentleman and I would be fine. I let the ponies lead the way and I followed, hoping my horse couldn't sense my anxiety. I'm sure he did, but as my boss said, he was a gentleman and a joy to ride. In fact he made me look good.

Following the youngsters down the lane, I felt sorry for my fellow workers. As usual, their ponies were jumpy, shying at every moving leaf, and when the proverbial motor bike zoomed past, there was the usual chaos. I sat on my steady, unfazed horse watching with sympathy.

On the way back to the yard I decided to try something. All the youngsters trotted into the yard eager for their breakfast, I urged Kerry to walk past the entrance. I assumed he would try to follow them, but to my surprise and delight he walked on. I rode about half a mile further on before turning round for home. Still he remained steady making no attempt to rush. I was amazed and when my boss asked me how I'd got on, I couldn't help enthusing. With that short ride my confidence slowly returned.

For the next few months I enjoyed looking after him … getting to know him and growing to love him. I wanted to show my affection, but he didn't like hugs or having his nose touched. However, I found if I offered him a treat, he would lower his head as if bowing before taking it.

When they took him hunting, I would wait eagerly for his return. When the horse box pulled into the yard I would call his name. He always responded with soft whickering sounds. It didn't matter how late they were getting back. I enjoyed feeding him and making sure he was dry and comfortable before leaving him for the night.

He was the first horse I ever had such a bond with and I know without a doubt he liked me. He had the sweetest nature and was a joy to ride, like a comfy rocking chair. If I had been more secure in my employment and more importantly if I'd had the money, I would have bought him. But sadly, it wasn't possible and when I was informed they were closing the yard and moving down south, I was heartbroken.

My boss was kind enough to find me another job. It was with a couple of ladies she knew who needed a stable hand. I said a tearful goodbye to everyone, especially Kerry and started my new job.

My new place was way in the country, surrounded by moorland. The yard was owned by two rather strange and not very friendly women. The horses were lovely. They bred and showed Dartmoor ponies, and also crossbred them with Arabs. It was an attractive combination.

The stabling was in the American style. A long barn with stables on both sides and a passage down the centre, it also incorporated the feed and tack room. Great when the weather was bad.

However, the women themselves were not

nice to me. At mealtimes they ignored me. In the evening I was forced to sit with them as my bedroom was basic and I had no money to buy books and even if I had, we were miles from anywhere. There were no shops. Sitting with them was decidedly frustrating. They would have the TV on, but without sound. As you can imagine most nights I went to bed early. Not a bad thing as after a long day, I was usually shattered.

I never got to ride and the food was sparse to say the least. The work was hard and the days long. I got so hungry, I would eat the pony's sugar cubes … not good for my teeth, but at least it gave me some energy.

As you can imagine I wasn't happy. I stayed for a few months and then gave them my notice. They didn't argue. After working a weeks' notice, I found myself at the bus stop with a small suitcase, my record player and whatever wages I was due.

Chapter 5

I had decided to go to London. I caught a bus to the local station and waited for a train. I had no idea what I was going to do. I just needed to get away from those two women and the lonely boring life I was being forced to live. I remember it was early in the morning when I arrived at Victoria station. I put my suitcase in left luggage and I wandered out of the station.

Having never been to a big city like London, I soon got lost and began to feel anxious. Men whistled at me as they drove by. Men on building sites did the same.

Being short of money, I needed to sell my

record player. I wandered the streets looking for some kind of pawn shop. By late afternoon I still had no success. As I wandered from street to street, the record player seemed to get heavier. Tired and hungry I began to panic. It would be dark soon and I was completely lost.

Close to tears I saw a policeman walking towards me. Not knowing what else to do I hurried up to him. He was nice and smiled as I told him my story. He told me to go with him to the police station. When we arrived he sat me down with a cup of tea, which was more than welcome. Taking my record player he offered me money for it, which I gladly accepted. I don't think he really wanted it. I believe he was just being kind. He told me his shift finished in a short while and then he would find me somewhere to stay.

I can still remember the relief I felt. Knowing I was safe and would get the help I needed, raised my spirits. With money in my pocket, a cup of hot tea and a chance to rest, I began to feel optimistic. The policeman true to his word drove me to the train station where I retrieved my case from left luggage. He then drove me to Kensington to a civil service hostel for women.

He told me he had enquired about a vacancy in the hostel. However, the lady who ran it seemed rather officious and not keen to let me stay, as I wasn't a civil servant.

Tired and frightened, I couldn't help myself I

began to cry. Fortunately, she took pity on me. I thanked the policemen, and then followed her upstairs to a room I would share with three other girls.

Looking back on this experience, I now know God had a hand in keeping me safe and providing for me. It was an experience I've never forgotten. I lived in the hostel for about two years ... a happy two years.

In the early sixties it was easy to find work. The stores on Oxford Street were always looking for staff. In those days you could walk into a store get a job and just as quickly leave and find work in another store. Basically, that's what I did, until I found the job I liked. I pretty much worked my way down the street and back up the other side.

However, eventually I found work in a coat shop. The merchandise went from expensive furs, like mink and fox, to cheaper sixties style rain wear. Being only eighteen, I was the youngest staff member. My employer often asked me to model the younger style coats and rainwear. It sometimes entailed leaving the shop and going to a photographic studio, I loved it.

My only problem working there was handling the till. Maths as I've said before was a no no. However, my sales skills and dealing with the customers was good. I would sell a coat and another member of staff would do the transaction for me, it worked well.

The lady who generally helped me became a close friend. Sometimes, at the weekend I would go and stay at her house. She had a lovely family. They always made me feel welcome. In some ways it was the family I always wanted. She became like a mother to me.

Some weekends she went to local clubs singing. I went with her. Watching her perform I decided I would love to do it myself. I wasn't sure how good my voice might be, but I wanted to try. I loved music and in the hostel I would join the other girls to watch Top of the Pops on the television.

Seeing my interest, my friend advised me to take singing lessons. She took me to her teacher. He listened to me sing and agreed to take me ... on the understanding I would not sing publically for two years, but would train with him and practise. I was thrilled and agreed without reservation.

During those two years I continued working in the shop and twice a week I went for my singing lessons. It was during that time I contracted a viral pneumonia. It was over Christmas. I can't say I had felt ill when I went to bed. The next morning, Christmas Eve, a friend was driving me home to my parents. It would be the first time I had been home for a long time.

When I woke I felt dreadful. I could hardly move and had a raging unquenchable thirst. Due to it being holiday time the hostel was pretty much empty. The girls I shared with had gone home. I managed to get downstairs to the dining room. Food was of no interest, but I nearly drank the tea ern dry. It was fortunate I had packed the night before, so all I had to do was wait for my lift.

I could see my friend looked concerned when he saw me. He was a nice guy ... a musician. Sadly I don't remember his name. On the journey home I managed to stay awake long enough to give him directions. But as soon as he pulled up outside my parent's house, I remember nothing more.

Mother told me, they carried me in and put me to bed. For four days over Christmas I was unconscious, with a high fever and delirious. It was fortunate my stepfather was a Doctor, but mother said it was a close thing for a while. He went back and forth to his surgery trying to find medication to help me. Eventually, I began to improve. But mother said the stress of the situation. The constant care put a strain on his heart. I was extremely grateful to him. Basically, he saved my life.

For me and for them, Christmas came and went. It was a good few weeks before I recuperated enough to return to the hostel. Once I got back, life carried on as normal. I worked in the shop and continued my singing lessons. The two years of training past quickly and one day when I arrived for my lesson, David my teacher told me he had booked me to do a summer show at The Winter Gardens in Morecombe.

It was a variety show, with the Dallas Boys,

Eve Boswell, the Tiller girls and numerous other acts. Max Bygraves topped the bill. I was part of a singing group, put together for the show. The show ran for the whole summer. I was in heaven. I adored my costume. It was a beautiful peach crinoline dress. Each of us girls wore different coloured dresses, the lead singer wore white.

That summer is special to me. Being part of the show was an amazing experience. It also enabled me to get my Equity card. But not only that, it was the year I became twenty one. My parents along with my sister came to see the show and to help me celebrate what was a perfect birthday. For the first time ever, I saw pride in their eyes. It felt good.

It was a sad day when the show came to an end and I said goodbye to the rest of the cast. Buzzing with excitement, I returned to London. Filled with hope, I eagerly anticipated what lay ahead for me. We all have dreams and for many of us things never quite turn out the way we expect or hope. However, I had fifteen years as a professional singer and I enjoyed every minute of it.

After the show in Morecombe, I sang in different clubs around London, with occasional times of resting as we called it, in between jobs. In 1968, I was booked to play the handmaiden to the princess in Aladdin, at The Bournemouth Pavilion Theatre. It stared Harry H Corbett. It was a great experience. I enjoyed working in Pantomime, they were always fun.

When the show finished, I returned to London and found myself resting again. During that time I found a small flat in Maida vale. Finding work took a while longer. However, after spending time perusing the Stage newspaper, I found work in Murry's a rather posh cabaret club just off Regent Street. Unbeknown to me, the club was known for its connection to the Profumo affair. Christine Keeler and Mandy Rice Davies had worked in the club. I hasten to add, it was before my time.

I wanted to sing, but there were no vacancy's at the time, so I agreed to join the dancers until a singing position became available. I can't say I enjoyed the dancing, not that you could call it that. The stage was so small all we could do was walk round in time to the music, which suited me as I couldn't dance anyway. For the opening and the finally numbers we were topless. At first I was horrified, but I got used to it, and to be honest once we put the highly decorative necklace on, it was hard to see anything.

It was a whole other world. But I made friends and grew fond of the lady who ran the club on behalf of the owner. She was kind and took care of me. Overtime, I was given my own late night singing slot with a pianist called Cliff and his drummer.

They were great musicians, and we worked well together. I danced in the two cabaret shows and then sang from three until four in the morning. I enjoyed it. Cliff was a great pianist and I got to sing all my favourite songs, mostly ballads as people at that time in the morning wanted the slow dances, or to sit and talk.

I worked in the club for a number of years and eventually along with my late night set, I also joined the show singers. There were two shows a night and we sang for both. There were four of us who sang with the orchestra. It was a cramped space and yet somehow it worked. Even the orchestra seemed to fit comfortably in their allotted space.

Once a year the show was changed and on Sundays we all turned up to rehearse. Anyone who didn't was fined. Considering it was a club, the rules were strict. Mondays we had to go to the hairdresser. The salon was booked by the owner of the club. It was free for us, but any girl who didn't go was again fined.

When rehearsing a new show, I found it fascinating how different the club looked in the daytime. At night with the soft lights and the plush red velvet seating, it looked so intimate and romantic, whereas in the daytime, it looked old and tired.

Working in the club was hard, it was a long night. We were there from nine at night, until around four in the morning.

But I enjoyed it. I had a repertoire of over a hundred songs that I knew by heart. When I left the club, my voice had matured and I had learned a lot and made some useful contacts. I remained friends with Cliff and we occasionally worked together.

For a few months after leaving the club there was little work to be found. I did some recording work for a radio station and some backing tracks for advertising. Many times I did extra work for different films at Pinewood Studios and for TV. I was an extra in many of the Doctor series on TV. I was also in a dark TV film called Brimstone and Treacle. I played the other woman!

In 1975 I played the princess in Aladdin in Welwyn Garden City, with Peter Denyer, Alan Vicars and a large cast of other characters.

When the pantomime season ended, I found myself resting again. By chance I met a friend from Murry's, Sadie. It was good to see her and catch up. We had grown quite close over the years I'd worked in the club. She told me the club had shut down. I was shocked and a little sad. I had spent many happy years working there. We met a few times after that and renewed our friendship.

Sadie was about the same age as me. She was beautiful and a lovely dancer. We joined forces and with help from Cliff my pianist, we put together an act ... calling ourselves Night and Day. We chose that as she had long blond hair and mine was long and dark. I did most of the singing and Sadie danced. It worked well and we enjoyed it. We worked the clubs and occasional restaurants around the west end.

We had a booking with other artists, and a band to go to the Tivoli Gardens in Denmark. We were there for the weekend. I can't say I enjoyed it much. Nevertheless, it was a good experience. When we returned to London we were offered cabaret work in a Japanese night club near Knightsbridge.

This proved to be long term and most enjoyable. There were two shows a night. Sadie and another girl Audrey danced, as I sang. Cliff and his drummer were with us, which was great. There was also a belly dancer. I learned to speak a bit of Japanese and even sang in Japanese, which went down extremely well. It was there I gained my love for Japanese food.

However, after a few years, the owner of the club informed us due to the cost, they were phasing out live music and so sadly they had to let us go. I was disappointed and sad, especially as the sort of work I liked to do was becoming scarcer by the day. Wherever, you went it was disco or piped music. You seldom saw live acts in any of the clubs.

Sadly, I lost contact with Cliff, the drummer and Audrey. I kept in touch with Sadie. On occasion we would meet in a wine bar and catch up. She had met someone and I could see it was serious. He was a nice guy. I went to their wedding and for a while that was the last time I saw her.

From then on finding work became harder. I

did odd bits here and there, but most of my time was spent drinking and drowning in depression and self-pity. I had always been an up or down person. Either the depths of despair, or hysterically happy, there was no in between.

My mood swings weren't so noticeable when I was busy working. I was doing what I loved, but once that stopped, I was forced to live with me. All the anger and baggage from my childhood, all the negative input from my family would resurface. Add to that, the insecurity and fear of not knowing how I was going to survive, without an income, scared me.

Yes I was on the dole, but it was hardly enough to pay the rent and eat. Not only that, being on the dole felt like I was confirming my parent's opinion of me. I was a loser and would not amount to much.

Most days I felt as though I was drowning in a thick black fog. It would lift for a while, but then return. Twice I tried to end my life. One time I nearly succeeded. I was rushed to hospital and had my stomach pumped, not a pleasant experience. While in hospital I was given some counselling. But all I wanted was to go home and drown my sorrows. Nothing had changed. I was still desperately unhappy and anxious.

It was during this time, I received a phone call from Aunty May. My mother and stepfather had moved up the Lake District. They lived in a small village called Arnside, not far from Kendal. My Aunt rang to tell me my stepfather had suffered a heart attack and had died. They had moved up to the Lake District as he wanted to retire near home. It was the place of his birth.

Unbeknown to me, it seems he was struggling with a heart problem. In reality moving to live up there was the worst decision he could have made. To a man with a heart problem, even the smallest hills are steep, and they had bought a house on the top of an extremely steep hill.

As I drove to the Lake District, I tried to imagine my mother's grief. I dreaded the state she was sure to be in. The man she loved had passed and she was alone. Still young, in her forties, what was she going to do?

When I arrived, aunty May greeted me. I could tell by her expression, things were understandably difficult. As best she could, she explained what had happened.

It would seem mother had gone with father to an AA meeting in Kendal. He had not felt particularly well during that day and when they got home he went to lie on the bed. Mother heard strange noises coming from the bedroom and rushed in. Just looking at him, she knew he was dying. Hearing the death rattles she screamed and shook him, sadly he was already dead.

My sister Margaret had moved with them to the Lake District. She'd found herself a live in job in a convalescent home just outside the village. But since the death of our stepfather she had stayed with mother. I had no idea where my brother was. None of us had heard from him in years. Mother had asked my Aunt to contact me.

Entering the house the wave of grief hit me. I had no idea what to say or do. Our relationship was still tense, but I loved her and seeing her grief and distress my heart filled with compassion.

It was lovely to see my sister. I know she was grateful I had come. My Aunt was wonderful. We would never have coped without her. She took over. Organizing the funeral arrangements and making sure everything ran as smoothly as possible.

The day of the funeral is a blur. One car and the hearse arrived outside the house. They both looked antiquated. I wondered how they managed to get up the hill. The hearse wasn't too bad, but the car for us was dreadful. It was like something out of a museum. I remember it smelt of oil and petrol. I was terrified once we were all in, it would roll backwards down the steep hill.

I remember my mother sobbing and not just at the funeral. She cried nonstop. None of us knew how to help her. Years later she told me how upset and angry she was about the vehicles and the actual funeral. Father had a circle of friends in the Lake District, but hardly anyone came to the service. It was a sad send off. Mother was deeply hurt. I believe it added to her distress.

Financially, my stepfather had left mother well provided for, she would never need to work. I returned to London hoping she would settle and make a new life for herself. Where she lived was beautiful. The modern house situated on a steep hill had amazing views over the beautiful Lakeland hills. Mother had my sister Margaret for company, along with her memories, but it wasn't enough.

Still young in her early forties, she continued to grieve and struggled with the concept of being alone. She was a woman who needed company … the company of a man. My sister kept me informed, and it soon became obvious mother couldn't cope on her own.

She started going to dances and meeting men. My sister became concerned. So I decided to leave London and return home. I think mother was grateful for the company.

I stayed for a while. Both mother and I went to work with my sister in the convalescent home. The money I earned enabled me to keep my flat on in London.

However, long story short I knew at some point I would return to London. Having discussed it with mother, she decided to put the house up for sale and come to London with me. My sister decided to stay, as she loved the Lake District and the convalescent home had accommodation for her. Not only that, she had met someone she liked.

Mother's house sold quickly and after a few

weeks I drove us to my flat in Maida Vale. I believe cutting all ties with a place that had meant so much to my stepfather … a place that held so many memories for mother, was a good thing.

* *
** **

It wasn't easy for her, living with me in my small flat. But then it wasn't easy for me either. However, it gave us the opportunity we needed to talk … a chance for me to discuss my childhood with all its hurt and pain. It was good to tell her how I felt and to hear her ask for forgiveness. It upset her to think how selfish and harsh she and my stepfather had been towards me and my brother.

It was a precious time of healing which we both needed. We had many such times, with numerous hugs and tears. Overtime, we grew close and established the relationship I had always wanted with her. We became mother and daughter, but more than that we became friends.

While living in the Lake District and struggling with her grief, she tried to find a new identity. She had bleached her hair blond. It looked awful … harsh and tarty. With gentle persuasion I managed to get her to a hairdresser, where it was returned to its normal colour, a soft brown.

It became obvious to us both. She couldn't

stay with me indefinitely. For a start, in the long term, my small flat could not accommodate us both. Not only that, she needed and wanted to make her own way in life.

Financially secure, and still young and attractive, she could live anywhere she liked. But we both knew living alone she would be lonely. Unlike me, a person who enjoys her own company, my mother needed companionship.

Rightly or wrongly, I contacted a respectable dating agency in the hope she might find someone to share her life with. Mother loved the idea. But in hindsight, I now realise it wasn't a good idea. We were given three contacts. One was a youngish man who lived in a bedsit … most unsuitable.

The second man was a little older than mother and had his own home in the country. He liked mother and was happy to travel up to London to meet with her. His wife had died and he told mother she could change the house in any way she wished. He was really keen. Unfortunately, mother said he had bad breath and it put her off. She talked me into going to the station and telling him she couldn't see him anymore. I felt awful. He was a nice man.

The third man she seemed to like. His name was Joseph. She insisted he reminded her of my stepfather. He was a train guard for London underground and lived in North London in a large rented flat. I wasn't so sure about him. I felt we should go back to the agency for more introductions. But mother liked him and they started going out together.

After a few months she moved in with him and his teenage daughter. Fortunately, they decided to live together as marring him would have meant losing the financial benefits left to her by my stepfather. For a while things were fine, but they soon began to unravel.

Too late mother realised she had made a mistake. He wasn't the man she thought he was. In a way he had tricked her. Leading her to believe he was something he wasn't. He had nothing to offer her and pretty soon she was looking for a place of her own, but it wasn't easy and she ended up staying with him.

Nevertheless, they got on reasonably well, probably because he was smitten with her. She on the other hand had little time for him. I suppose she felt cheated. She could have blamed me, as I instigated the agency idea, but she didn't. I had suggested going back to the agency for new introductions, but she refused, convinced initially that he reminded her of my stepfather. To me there was no resemblance at all. I believe because of her grief, she was subconsciously looking for Doctor Rodman and in appearance this man reminded her of him. So for better or worse, she stayed with him.

Chapter 6

As time passed mother seemed settled with Joseph. Mostly she seemed happy, or as happy as she could be under the circumstances. If nothing else Joseph was a kind man and he was extremely fond of mother. They were getting on with their lives.

I on the other hand, continued to struggle with life. Drinking heavily and fighting the demon of depression. It felt as though I was drowning. I'd lost a lot of weight. The hardness of my heart, the sort of life I had lived showed on my face. Not that I'd particularly lived a debauched life. But I had lived a full life and on my terms.

Filled with anger and distrust of men, I used them in any way I could. On occasion, I could be cruel to anything or anyone. I was not a nice person. I was lost and tormented. All through my singing career I had men friends, but I never let them come close. I set the boundaries and if they tried to cross, that was it, bye bye.

However, one man came close to softening my heart. His name was Peter. He used to come to Murry's with business friends. I had known him for a while, but lost contact. Then one night, he came to the Japanese club where I was singing. I was pleased to see him and we went out for a few months.

Initially, I hadn't realised he was seriously ill, until one day, he told me he only had a short time to live. I was devastated, as I had grown fond of him. He said he couldn't see me anymore. I know he was trying to protect me. He promised he would ring me, to say goodbye. He kept that promise. Over the phone he sounded so weak and breathless. He couldn't talk for long. It was distressing. After that phone call, I heard nothing more from him.

A month or so later I received a call. It was a friend of Peters. He told me that before Peter died, he asked this friend to contact me. It troubled Peter that due to circumstances, I was unable to attend his memorial service. He wanted his friend to take me to the church where he was buried.

We drove to the village where Peter and I had spent happy times together. His friend bought me lunch and afterwards he drove me to the church. He took me to Peter's grave and left me to spend some time alone.

It was a sad day. Peter was so ill, and yet he thought about me. He knew I would want to say goodbye. I was grateful that Peter's friend honoured his wish. Good friends are hard to find and so are good men and Peter was one of those. It was a privilege, even for a short time to know him.

As for the other men in my life, they came and went. I made sure to be the one who did the rejecting, not them. I know being rejected by my father and my stepfather, played a huge part in making me who I was. My mother's dislike of me when I was young didn't help.

Being introvert by nature, it was no strange thing I became a loner. As such, I escaped the rejection of others, but I could not escape myself. Hence the constant downward spiral ... the black cloud of despair and self-pity, followed by bouts of hysterical unreal happiness. I was at the mercy of myself, fighting my own demons and rapidly losing the battle.

Suicide was an option I took, twice. The first time was a half-hearted cry for help. A friend helped me through it. The second time I meant it. I ended up in hospital having my stomach pumped ... an extremely unpleasant and painful experience. Not only that, when Doctors and nurses know you have tried to take your own life, they are not overly sympathetic. They weren't to me, anyway.

I'm sharing this because of the wonderful miracle God accomplished in my life.

..
** **

In November 1981 my life changed for ever. As I have said, I was in a sorry state and things were coming to a head. I had come to a crossroad and I had no idea where to go and worse, no desire. I was scared to die and scared to live.

It was strange, before my friend Sadie got married, on the occasional nights we weren't working. We used to sit in my flat, watch the late night horror films, eat huge jacket potatoes and get drunk.

For some strange reason during these evenings we would read a bible. I had an old one given to me when I was very young by a lady in the Salvation Army.

Sadie and I always turned to Revelation. We had no understanding of the book, but I particularly was fascinated by the Lambs book of life ... I knew my name wasn't in it and I confess it bothered me.

I understand now, why I was so affected by Revelation. I believe even as a young child, inside me there was a seed of spiritual awareness. When I was unhappy or angry, I would cry out to God, "Why was

I born? I didn't ask to be born." As a child and young person, I knew nothing about God, only what we learned in the Convent and that didn't interest me in the least. Yet somehow I was conscious of God, enough to shout at Him in my distress.

As a child I was so unhappy. It must have showed on my face, because when I walked down the street, some people I past would look at me and say, "Cheer up, it's not the end of the world."

To me it was. Knowing I was unwanted … knowing the people who should have loved me, didn't, fostered insecurity and fear. As I grew up, I struggled with a deep lack of self-worth. My biggest desire was to make my mother proud of me. I thought then she might love me. But as I found out, it doesn't work like that.

Mother told me when I was little; sometimes she couldn't bear to look at me. Little things about me annoyed her, like when she needed me to blow my nose, and instead I would sniff. Or the times she dressed me in trousers and I kept pulling them up for no apparent reason. However, the thing she hated most was my lack of eye contact. But then, I say again, why would I want to look into the face of someone who hated me?

There are many forms of abuse, some worse and more destructive than others. The abuse I received was mild in comparison to what some poor children suffer, especially these days.

The abuse I suffered was not physical, but

emotional. I can honestly say, I don't remember my mother ever hugging or kissing me. I was kept at a distance. So too was my brother.

Only later in life, was I able to find and release the buried child within me, and no I'm not exaggerating! As a little one filled with insecurity and fear, you either go under, or as in my case you bury or hide anything considered weak, like emotion. Build a brick wall around your heart, then stand up and fight your corner and I mean fight. It's what I did and I'm here to prove it.

However, sometimes what is buried no matter how deep, has a habit of surfacing when you least expect it. In 1965 a boyfriend took me to see 'The Greatest Story Ever Told.' I was mesmerized and spent pretty the whole film in tears. I've never forgotten it. I had no idea why. But without exaggeration, I didn't just cry, I sobbed uncontrollably, much to the annoyance and embarrassment of the guy I was with.

Seeing Jesus life and final suffering was all I could think about. I left the guy standing in the street and went back to the hostel. The film pulled emotion from me I didn't know existed. All I wanted to do was be on my own to try and understand why I felt the way I did and why I couldn't stop crying.

Another time in the late sixties, I went to a Billy Graham crusade. Overcome with emotion, I responded to the invitation to give my life to Jesus. I was genuine. Again something had touched my heart. However, no one followed up my decision. Not knowing what to do next, I simply carried on with the life I knew, which was singing in Murry's cabaret club. But unbeknown to me, a seed had been planted.

Some years later, in the early eighties I had reached a crossroads in my life. I was going nowhere … nowhere good anyway. Desperate, I started to search, for what I wasn't sure. At the time I didn't understand that God was calling me to Himself.

I decided to go to the Church of England down the road from where I lived in Maida Vale, but after the service I left feeling just as empty.

A friend I had grown close to over the years was a Buddhist. Happy to help, she took me to one of her meetings. It wasn't for me and I left as quickly as I could.

Not knowing what to do, I became agitated. I was desperate, there had to be more to life than what I was experiencing. I determined I would search until I found what I was looking for. Somehow I knew I would recognize it. Don't ask me how, but I just knew I was being guided.

In a corner of my small flat I made an altar. I erected a small cross, bought some flowers, and put them in a vase. Each day I would kneel in front of this small altar and try to pray. I was unsure who I was praying to, and I had no idea what to say. I remember I cried a lot.

I knew nothing about being saved or born again. However, I knew without a doubt, that what or who I was looking for would not be found in Buddhism, or any other ism for that matter.

For weeks I knelt in front of my little altar, becoming more and more desperate. One day I was with my mother. She knew how unhappy I was and I know she worried about me. We were chatting and I was trying to explain how I felt, as talked I remembered Ron. He was a close friend of Josephs and would often stay with them for a meal. If I was there I noticed he always said grace. Obviously, mother noticed as well, but thought nothing of it. Seeing how unhappy I was, she suggested I have a talk with Ron. She felt he might be able to help.

So when Ron came to see Joseph, I approached him. I think he was taken aback, but it helped to talk to him. Unable to answer all my questions, he suggested I speak to a pastor friend of his. I was more than willing.

A week later he brought his friend to mother's flat. Desperate and unable to understand what I was looking for. I fired questions at him. I remember he sat in the chair opposite me with a cup of tea. He spoke gently about the love of Jesus. He answered my questions, but kept repeating the fact that Jesus loved me. He said it was obvious that Jesus was pursuing me. His soft words had me in floods of tears. I didn't understand everything he said, but I felt at last I was on the right track. This man had the answer and could help me.

He told us that on the following evening a

large crusade was being held in Brixton. He asked if we would like to go. Without hesitation I answered yes. Mother agreed to come with me. I'm not sure she understood what was going on, but neither did I really. I was searching and deep down I felt this could be the answer. I didn't realise it at the time, but God's timing is always perfect.

The next evening as I sat in his car, my stomach did flips of nervous excitement. I hardly noticed the sights of London as we drove to Brixton. Although, there was one important question I asked him. 'Can people drink in your church?' By this time I was a heavy drinker, drowning my sorrows most nights.

He was wise in the way he answered. He didn't really say yes or no, and as we got closer to Brixton, I forgot about it. Seeing the crowds of people my heart hammered with excitement and expectation. He led us inside and found some seats near the front.

The large building was full of West Indian people. They knew the pastor we were with and came to greet him. I can imagine what they thought as they looked at me, a thin worldly looking white woman, dressed inappropriately for church and yet the love they showed me and my mother took our breath away. I think among the hundreds of people there, we were the only white faces. Nevertheless, the acceptance and the feeling of being in the right place threatened to overpower me. At last I knew, in this place I would find what I was searching for.

Through most of the service I cried. The amazing singing … the powerful atmosphere contributed to my emotional state. Guy Notice, the preacher spoke with passion. To me it was as if I was the only person in that auditorium. He said everything I needed to hear. It was as though he knew me and knew about my life. I was transfixed. Hardly able to breath, I let the tears fall. When the altar call was made I wanted to respond, but somehow I couldn't leave my seat. I was so scared. I sat there trembling.

The pastor offered to take me to the front, but mother took my hand and we went up together. We knelt in the choir pews. A lady led me in what I now know was the sinners prayer. She prayed for me, but all I remember is crying. I don't think I'd ever cried so much in my life. I couldn't stop and I had no idea why. I was a trembling wreck. I clutched the small St John's book she gave me and just stood where I was. I had no idea what to do, but one thing I did know. I was not moving from that spot until I found what I was searching for. For me this was literally a matter of life or death. I had reached the end of myself. I knew if I left that building without finding the answer I sought, that would be it!

In the background I could hear the murmur of voices praying and soft music. I later found out it was an old hymn, 'Just as I Am.' Over the years it's become a favourite.

As I stood there waiting, for what, I wasn't sure. I glanced up and all of a sudden it was as if a beautiful glowing ball of light came through the roof of the building and flew into the congregation. It happened so fast.

I felt a thrill of excitement. I remember turning to my mother and saying, "He's here, He's here." Somehow, I knew the ball of light was God. In that moment the place erupted, it was awesome. People cried and fell to the ground. I could hear loud prayers. It sounds as though it was chaotic, but it wasn't. It was amazing and strangely I felt part of it ... felt at peace. I knew God had entered the building.

Gradually, it went quiet and people returned to their seats. I stayed where I was. I could see people putting on their coats ready to leave. I couldn't move. I was desperate, but for what? I wasn't sure. Nevertheless, I wasn't moving until it happened.

Mother stood with the pastor. "It's time to leave," she said.

Disappointed, I reluctantly left the pews and walked towards her. It was then my legs began to feel weak and shaky, like jelly. A lady took my arm and asked if I was alright. I said yes, but told her my legs felt strange. She said I should sit down and guided me towards a chair, but I didn't make it. All of a sudden I felt a warm wind come into my throat. I could hardly breathe. It felt like it swirled around my entire body, from my head to my toes. The love

I felt was so powerful, it took my breath away.

Unable to stand, I crumpled to the floor. It was the most beautiful sensation, but I admit I was frightened. Yet at the same time an awesome sense of peace overwhelmed me. A group of ladies gathered around me, giving encouragement. They told me it was the Lord Jesus and I should praise Him, which I did, while at the same time calling for my mother.

When the beautiful wind left me, I was legless and had to be helped to my feet. The pastor and my mother managed to get me to his car. All the while I was laughing and crying. To others it must have looked like I was drunk, but as the bible says. I was drunk in the spirit. Not that I understood that at the time. I was just so full of joy and peace. I wanted to go around Brixton telling everyone that Jesus was alive.

From that day, 3rd of November 1981 my life changed completely. Later, mother told me when I called for her, my voice sounded like it did when I was a child. She rushed over and stood with the ladies staring at me.

A few days later we were talking about it, and she said that as she looked at me, it was as though my face, initially so hard and troubled was being changed and softened before her eyes. Who needs cosmetic surgery when you meet with the living God? This experience had a profound effect on her, which I will explain later.

At the time I had no idea what was happening to me, but the joy I felt was overwhelming. All the fears and worries I had carried into that building seemed to have fallen away. I felt clean and wonderfully free ... I felt like a child. In that moment Jesus had cleansed and saved my life, literally. Praise God.

I will never forget it. Every wonderful detail will remain forever in my mind. It holds me steady and keeps my faith strong. To know I am loved by almighty God, the creator of the universe is a mind blowing thought. He met me at my weakest point.

He didn't come to me as I stood in the pews. I knew He was there in the building and I didn't want to leave. Sad and scared for my future, I took that step away from the pews and into His waiting arms. I was embraced and breathed upon by the living God. To know that Jesus was alive and tangible was too wonderful for words. I wanted to tell all the people in Brixton ... Jesus is alive. I was so excited.

From that night everything in my life changed, some things instantly, others over time. I really was a new creature. Life had meaning now, Jesus had saved me ... forgiven me. No more fear, no more searching. I was loved, I was safe.

I remember the next day going for a walk around Willesden, where mother and Joseph lived. It's not the nicest part of London. However, as I walked around, I couldn't help smiling at everyone I passed. All the trees looked greener. In fact colours appeared sharp and bright. Bird song sounded more beautiful. It was as though every one of my senses had suddenly come to life.

I floated around those grubby streets, overwhelmed by the amazing miracle that had taken place in my life. In the space of one night I had become a different person. No longer confused and lost. No longer would I need to stand in front of a mirror and ask, 'Who am I?" I knew. I was a born again child of God.

* *
** **

A few months after becoming a Christian, I left my Maida Vale flat and moved in with mother and Joseph. I spent most days with them anyway, so it was decided I should live there. It was just as well as singing work had dried up and financially I was beginning to struggle.

Spiritually I was under attack, especially in my flat. I had lived there for many years and suffice to say I'd had many experiences good and bad.

On one particular occasion I got home from a church meeting and went to bed. I had a bad dream … more of a nightmare. Actually, I wasn't sure if I was asleep or awake. But something heavy was sitting on my chest and the room was filled with evil beings. The language was foul really disgusting. With the weight of the thing on my chest I struggled to breathe. Nevertheless, I fought to shout the name of Jesus and eventually the evil left. Even as a very young Christian, I knew His name had the power to free me.

Terrified I lay trembling under the covers. I felt the Lord directing me to get my bible. At first I was too scared to get out of bed, but I did and quickly carried the bible back to bed. He took me to Luke 17 verse 5 which was amazing. It's the scripture where the disciples ask Jesus to give them more faith.

I felt the presence of Jesus really powerfully in my room and cried as I read the word. Not only did it comfort me with regard to the spiritual attack, but also, I realised I shouldn't worry about finances, or anything else for that matter, but just to have faith and trust in Jesus. When I closed the bible and lay down, I slept well.

Joseph had kindly turned the spare room in his flat into a small bedsit for me. I spent most of my time in prayer and reading my bible. I set up a small altar in the corner of the room and used it to centre my thoughts. Jesus had saved me and cleansed me from all my sins. I was overcome with gratitude. It was almost too much to take in ... I was forgiven. All

I wanted to do was praise Him.

Overtime, I learned I didn't need an altar. All He wanted was my heart of worship. But as a young Christian it helped me express my love for Him. I was short of money, but each week I would buy flowers for Him and put them on the altar. It was my small sacrifice of love.

The pastor who had taken me to Brixton invited us to join his church. I was more than happy to do so. I was so on fire I couldn't wait to get to church each Sunday and any meeting in the week, of which there were plenty.

The New Testament Church of God has a strict dress code. Ladies must wear hats and dresses or skirts. Trousers are not allowed, neither is make up or jewellery. It came as a bit of a shock, but I was so in love with the Lord Jesus, I happily complied. After the rather wild life I had led this was good for me.

I had little understanding of biblical modesty and many times in meetings I would be helped to the front of the church to be prayed for. For years I had never worn a bra, I hated them. However, one Sunday, it was as though a voice quietly said, "Yvonne, you need to buy a bra." Yes, He did use my name, and yes, those were the words I heard. I remember it so clearly, because it totally took me by surprise. Not least because it was further confirmation that the God I now served, was tangible and alive.

In the New Testament Church of God, which was the first church I attended after being saved. I met a young man called Winston. Once a week he would take a group of us to a prayer meeting. They were brilliant. I immersed myself in the power of God. The sense of freedom in these meetings was wonderful and these days it's something I truly miss.

Winston was fascinated by end time teaching. I learned a lot from him. He introduced me to a marvellous young preacher called Roger Price. I soaked up every tape I could get my hands on.

I loaned them to my friend Sadie. I had told her about my experience in Brixton and I knew it affected her. I was thrilled when some months later she told me she had given her heart to the Lord. It seems when she heard my testimony and listened to the tapes I gave her, she decided to go to her local church. A young man there led her to the Lord. God is so good.

I was thriving spiritually, God presence was so close. We were inseparable, it felt awesome. One Monday evening we attended the prayer meeting. We finished praying and the Pastor was about to speak to us. As I sat there, I felt the presence of God come upon me.

Before going further, I need to explain that

ever since giving my heart to the Lord in Brixton, I had spent hours in prayer pleading with Him to take me home. As I've already shared. From a young age, I was never truly happy.

Having met and fallen in love with Jesus, my heart's desire was to be with Him. I was truly a spiritual baby with no knowledge of spiritual things. All I knew was I had met the most wonderful person in the world. He loved me and I wanted to be with Him. And I was going to pester Him until He took me, which I did, with a lot of crying and pleading.

On this particular night in church, I fell under the power of God. I could not stop trembling, it was such a wonderful feeling, but at the same time a little frightening. I felt myself go down in the pews. I vaguely felt hands lifting me out and taking me to the front of the church, where I began to praise and worship God.

I knelt and rested my arms on the altar rail. I was facing the pulpit. The décor of the church was dark wood, from the panelling on the walls to the pews. The large pulpit was also dark wood … intricately carved. My eyes were closed and yet I could see the pulpit. As I knelt in worship it was as though I was no longer in church, but in another world. Spiritually, I felt alert. Suddenly, a light appeared as if from the pulpit … an all-encompassing golden light.

As I watched, from out of this light Jesus appeared. The vision of Him is embedded in my mind. I now realise as a mature Christian, what I was seeing was a spiritual vision, but at the time it was as though he was there in person. It was a profound and unforgettable experience.

He was so tall. His face was shrouded in gold, also His white clothing. There were sandals on His feet. At the time I was convinced I saw His eyes. Spiritually, I did. They were dark and looked at me with such love.

He held out His arms, I could see the wounds in His hands. The feeling of love was so strong it overpowered me. It rolled over me like waves. My heart pounded. I can't explain what it was like, there are no words. I wanted to stay there with Him for ever. Holding out my arms to Him, I struggled to breath and waited with anticipation, convinced He would take me. But then He spoke. He said one word, "PATIENCE."

I admit I was surprised, and I confess disappointed, especially as over time I have learned how important patience is. When you struggle with a lack of it as I do, it's even harder. I have never been a patient person, so the message was hard.

Nevertheless, being in His presence was awesomely wonderful. I said with conviction. "I will Lord, I will." Tears streamed down my face. His presence was so powerful. I have never forgotten it, and I never will.

No one will ever tell me I didn't see Jesus and hear His voice. I know I did. I didn't realise at the time, but Joseph was kneeling beside me. Later he told me that he knew I had experienced something profound ... that I had seen something. That was a blessed confirmation for me.

Jesus is awesome and so beautiful.

Chapter 7

Eventually, the pastor found out that mother and Joseph were not married. They told him it was their choice, but he insisted if they wished to remain in fellowship they must marry. Joseph was a Christian. My mother after seeing the change in me gave her life to the Lord. So rather than disobey the pastor, they agreed. For mother it was more about pleasing God. However, she wasn't happy about it for many reasons. One of them being it would hit her financially. Getting married meant she would lose some of the inheritance my stepfather had left her. But like me she knew she must trust God.

The wedding was arranged in secret. I felt it was an ironic twist. Mother had to marry my step farther, the man she loved in secret. Now, she was forced to marry Joseph, in secret. The pastor didn't want the congregation to know mother and Joseph were living together. So early in the morning on the day of the wedding we arrived with Joseph's friend Ron. The church was devoid of light, the curtains were drawn. There would be no guests and no music. Ron and I were the witness.

Mother was not happy, the last thing she wanted to do was marry Joseph. He on the other hand seemed delighted. I sang Amazing Grace for them and then we left in the same clandestine way we had arrived. No one in the church ever found out. But I think it was a sad day for mother. It was certainly a sad and depressing wedding. I felt for her.

On Monday evenings there was always a prayer meeting at the church. This particular Monday we had fasted. During the meeting I felt the presence of the Lord telling me I must be baptised. I felt anxious and confused as we were to go through the waters of baptism in a few weeks' time.

Fortunately, some of the ladies in the church explained that probably the Lord meant for me to be filled with the Holy Spirit. The thought filled me with happiness and excitement. It was a good meeting and I felt blessed.

A few weeks later on a Saturday evening, along with a number of other people, my mother and I went through the waters of baptism. It was a blessing to watch my mother be baptised.

After the sadness and trauma of my childhood, it was wonderful to have such closeness with her. It was something I had always wanted. It took many years, but God did it. Nothing is too hard for Him. The next day, Sunday, we were to be accepted into full membership of the church. I have so much to thank Him for.

I continued to dwell on Gods words about spiritual baptism. A few weeks had passed since my water baptism. Then one day we heard that a crusade would be taking place in a church down the road. I felt God wanted me to go there. Mother and I went together with a few of our church brethren.

The church building was smaller than ours and it was filled to capacity. For the crusade they had a visiting preacher. He was brilliant. I listened intently to every word he said. He preached on the crucifixion. The presence of God was powerful. I so wanted to be filled with the Spirit and when the time came for prayer the power of God was awesome. I confess to being nervous ... unsure what to expect.

However, the visiting minister called a halt to the evening, as people were becoming over excited and noisy. He said, 'In the presence of the Holy Spirit everything should be done decently and in order.' We were told to go home and return the following evening, Sunday. Even though things had not gone as I expected, nevertheless I felt at peace.

I could hardly wait for Sunday evening. My anticipation was sky high. God had told me I must do this, so I had no doubt it was going to happen. It was a brilliant service. The visiting preacher continued to speak about Jesus suffering on the cross and how at the same time the curtain in the temple was torn from top to bottom giving entrance to all, allowing those who trust in Christ, to go into Gods presence.

Because of Jesus sacrifice, we have been made acceptable to God. It's an awesome truth, as he preached I wept. Because of Jesus, mankind could now approach the throne of God. Through most of his preaching I wept. The presence of God was strong upon me.

He called those who wished to receive the Holy Spirit to come to the front. I was among the first. This time everyone remained quiet and reverent. It was a wonderful atmosphere.

He laid his hands on my head and told me to receive the baptism of the Holy Spirit and praise God. I opened my mouth and praised, but not in my normal tongue. God had blessed me with a prayer language. Slumping to my knees I joined others in praise of our awesome God. It was a beautiful night. I was filled with joy when we left to go home.

** **

A month or so later we went to our usual Monday prayer meeting. This particular night we were to share Holy Communion, only it didn't happen. The Holy Spirit took control. He kept taking me to the table. Praying in tongues, I walked around it touching the elements.

I wish there had been an interpretation, because at the time I had no idea why I was doing it. I just knew I must. No one in the congregation including the pastor moved or said anything. That night there was no communion. It was a strange evening and one I continue to remember. Only a year or so later did I understand why I was urged to do what I did.

Chapter 8

In May 1982 we went to see my sister Margaret and her husband Fred. She met him while working at the convalescent home. Margaret's husband was a gardener. He also worked at the convalescent home. They had married a few years before I became a Christian.

This short holiday was the first time we had seen them in quite a while. Her husband Fred was now the head gardener for one of the National Trust properties. It was a beautiful place. They and their three year old son Ben lived in a lovely house belonging to the Trust.

They lived well, it was a different life to my own and I confess envy raised its ugly head and latent insecurity again plagued me. I felt I had nothing and had achieved nothing. My sister appeared to have it all. They even had a horse. Whereas I, a grown woman was basically living with my parents, I felt a failure … worse a jealous failure.

In the evening after having our meal, I went for a walk in the beautiful grounds. Most days the property is open to the public. But in the evening it's closed and I had the place to myself. It was a lovely spring evening, the only sound, bird song.

I was so caught up in envy and self-pity. I was unaware of anything else. The Lords voice took me by surprise. I wept as I heard the words; **in my father's house are many mansions**. John 14 verses 1 – 3. My tears were now, tears of praise.

Maybe I didn't have what my sister had. However, my future was assured. I had the love of Almighty God. My sister had only what this world has to offer and it's temporal. My tears were also for her and her family.

I had taken the opportunity to share my testimony with her. She listened and being of a soft nature, I do believe she took on board what I said. For now it was up to me to show Jesus in my life and to keep praying for them both, which I did.

On the journey home to London, I said nothing to mother about my experience in the garden. I felt it was between me and the Lord. God's grace poured out and another lesson learned. I have to constantly remind myself. I am no longer of this world. I am a pilgrim passing through. I'm still learning to hold onto the things of this world lightly. This is not my home.

* *

In July 1982 I was privileged to go to Israel. In fact, looking back 1982 turned out to be a pivotal year in my spiritual walk. I had only been a Christian a few months, when a kind friend invited me to join an Elim church group that were going to Israel. Knowing nothing about Israel and the Jewish people, I jumped at the chance.

I had an awesome time and learned so much. Our base for the ten days was the youth hostel in Jerusalem, across the road was the King David hotel. Our accommodation was basic but clean and comfortable. The actual building is built of white stone, classic in design and extremely attractive. From the outside it looks posher than it is, but I loved it. I was just so thrilled and excited to be in Israel.

Adding to my joy, the first night of our arrival, an American Christian group called the Continental singers, were performing in a small theatre situated in the grounds of the hostel. Their performance was wonderful. For me it was the icing on the cake. I felt as though I had gone to Heaven.

My time in Israel was filled with amazing sights and sounds and huge emotional moments. I particularly enjoyed exploring the old city. The sights and the smells of the different spices was a treat for my senses, but also a real culture shock.

I remember strolling down one narrow cobbled street and hearing a young man shouting. Stepping aside I looked in the barrow as he hurried past. It was full of sheep's heads. Blood dripped onto the street, hence his warning shouts to get out of the way.

Another time again in the old city, we were making our way to the church of the Holy Sepulchre. Being at the rear of our group, I noticed a man walk passed me. He stopped and looked back, I followed his gaze. There was a beautiful little lamb, sniffing around an old door. I went towards it with my hand out. But the shepherd called it. The lamb ignored me and ran after him.

It reminded me of Jesus' words. 'My sheep hear my voice and follow me.' It was a wonderful illustration of the truth of God's word. That lambs only interest was the shepherd.

Being in Israel helped me to get a deeper understanding of the scriptures. Why Jesus preached as He did. The parables He used and His frequent teachings about sheep and shepherding. In Israel sheep are not driven, they follow the shepherd. It was fascinating to see it in reality.

Experiencing all of this opened my mind, gave me a better understanding and a greater desire to study God's word. I love Israel and the thought that in some places my feet trod in my saviour's footsteps was emotional and mind blowing.

I felt at home and when the time came to leave I was miserable. I really didn't want to go home. On the morning we were to leave, I woke early and finished my packing. Sitting on my bed I watched the sun rise. Going to the window, I could see the walls of the old city. The stone work glowed gold in the early morning light. It was beautiful.

I couldn't stop the tears and prayed for God to help and strengthen me. When I finished I got my bible and turned the pages. I felt the Lord stop me. My tears fell freely when I read the scripture. It was Luke 8 v 39, the passage where Jesus has delivered the demonic man who lived among the tombs. He wants to go with Jesus, but the Lord refuses and tells him to go home and tell his friends what great things God has done for him.

My tears now were tears of wonderment and joy. Being a young Christian I was still learning the scriptures and this was one I didn't know. To say I was overawed was an understatement! I knew God had heard and answered my prayer. I felt blessed and at peace, content to return home and share my wonderful experiences.

No matter the circumstances in our lives, if we let Him, God will help and guide us. When we are weak, He is strong.

* *
** **

A few months after returning from Israel, I went to Bible College in Northampton. It was something I wanted to do. Financially, I could never have afforded the cost, but the church helped and supported me. I was truly grateful to all the members for their financial support.

It was my desire to learn more about the bible and grow closer to the Lord. I felt it was what He wanted me to do. Actually, I learned more about myself than I did about theology. Nevertheless, it wasn't a wasted year. Lessons were learned and I grew spiritually.

The college was a new venture for the New Testament Church of God. Initially, there were only a few of us students. But everything has to start somewhere. In many ways it was a good year and fun to be a path-finder so to speak. The first I hope of many future students.

I had been a Christian nine months when I went to the college. In those nine months the Lord and I were inseparable. His presence was tangible. It felt as though all I had to do was call and He would be there for me. It was an amazing and beautiful time. I love Him dearly and I knew without a doubt,

He loved me. He was the father I never had. I learned to be a child, trusting, happy and for the first time ever ... secure.

However, one morning when I woke, I knew something was different. It felt as though He had left me. I was bereft. The whole morning I moped around, lost and feeling abandoned. Was He going to be like every other man in my life?

In the afternoon there were no classes so I lay on my bed depressed and tearful. Jesus, the one whom I loved had left me. That's how it felt.

Later, one of the other students came into my room. 'Read this,' she said handing me a book. I looked at her. 'It's time to grow up. The honey moon is over.' I felt her words were harsh, how did she know what I was going through. However, when I read the book, or should I say devoured it. I realised she did. I was amazed ... it was my experience!

It was a story written by a messianic Jew. His experience was the same as mine. For nine months He and Jesus were inseparable. Just like me it was as though Jesus was at his beck and call. I understood completely.

Like me, one morning he woke and it was as if the Lord had left him. Apparently, he drove his Christian friends mad with his tears and confused questions. They told him the same as my fellow student told me. 'The honey moon is over, it's time to grow up and stand on your own two feet.'

We have to learn to grow in our faith, trust

Him and walk the path He has set before us. We are to be warriors not children. He has promised never to leave us or forsake us. Our relationship with Him our trust grows stronger as we mature.

The book he wrote was brilliant. Sadly, I can't remember the title, or the author's name. Nevertheless, it was a huge help to me. Father had not left me, He never would. No longer would I take faltering baby steps, now I must stride bravely into the fray, proclaiming Jesus is Lord.

I remember one evening in early December. Seven of us attended the prayer meeting in the college chapel. At the time an American evangelist was staying at the college. During the meeting he prayed for all of us. He prayed for me and told me. "I must be humble and submit my life completely, if the Lord is to use me."

I didn't fully understand his words and felt a little disturbed and upset. Quietly, I asked God if the words really were from Him. The evangelist returned and laid his hands on me again. This time he said, "The Lord cannot be the same with you as He was." Amazed at his words, I silently thanked God. Only I knew the sort of relationship the Lord and I had shared for a good nine months … the incredible closeness. So I knew God was speaking to me through this man.

He went on to say. "I will be led as a lamb to the slaughter and He wants me to witness to my family and friends. He has a work for me to do, but again I must humble myself."

It was an amazing and wonderful meeting. My desire is to be the person God wants me to be. I know I can't do anything myself. I have to trust and wait on the Lord. That goes for all of God's people.

*** ***

On occasion the minister from my church would come to the college and see me. He would bring a gift from the members, check I was alright and pray for me. I appreciated it.

The first college year was nearly over and we were all preparing for the summer break. It was during this rather hectic time that I heard the sad and disturbing news. It shook me to my core. I was saddened and at the same time angry. It would seem the minister of our church had been having a relationship with a member of the congregation. It had been going on for years. His wife was American and they had two children.

The woman involved in the relationship wanted to end the affair, but it seems he didn't, so she hid a tape recorder under the bed and it all came out. It was horrible and so sad for his wife. She took the children and returned to America. The minister was thrown out of the church. It was an awful situation and a shock to everyone.

I was reminded of the night in church, the night I walked round the communion table touching the elements. I had no idea why and the minister made no attempt to stop me. Now I understood why.

What made it worse for me was the fact he had insisted my mother marry Joseph, while all the time he was having an affair. I couldn't get my head round it. I felt hurt and angry. I know mother felt the same. Believe me, I'm not condoning mother and Joseph living together. But they had been pressured and given no opportunity to seek God.

Before the minister intervened I was trying to help mother find somewhere to live as she wanted to leave Joseph. Having become a Christian herself she felt more confident and prepared to live her own life. But once they were married she felt she should stay and make the best of it.

Hearing what the minister had done, a man we had trusted and respected threw her into a depression. She felt she had been tricked and coerced into a marriage she didn't want and in a way it was true. It was an awful time for us all.

I felt for Joseph, he was a quiet man and didn't say much, but I'm sure he was hurt and affected by the situation. He was fond of mother and secretly I think he was grateful the minister forced them to marry. However, in the long run, they were never really happy. Even now, I'm not sure it was Gods will for them to marry.

I believe from my own life, even if we take a

wrong path, God will still bring good out of a bad situation. In all our lives there are lessons we have to learn. Humility, graciousness and love I believe are paramount in a marriage, from both parties.

Joseph was a weak man, but he was not a bad man, if mother had tried to meet him half way, perhaps they could have been happier. Nevertheless, it's not for me to criticise.

Suffice to say the situation had been taken out of their hands and they were forced to follow a path that turned out to be hard for them both. But bitterness is a root best avoided. Many a life is destroyed by it, as I almost found out to my cost.

I expected to remain at the college and complete the three year course. However, I struggled during that first year. Not so much academically, but because a personal situation made my life difficult. So I made the hard decision to leave, even though a kind family member offered to pay my fees for the next two years. But with circumstances the way they were, I had to refuse their kind offer. It was a relief when I left. Two people alone knew what I had been through, God and my mother.

To be honest I would have struggled as the terms progressed, as I am not the best student in the world. In that first year in spite of the difficulties I learned a lot, although it was more about me than theology and sadly, it was not all good. But it was an experience and in hindsight positive. One lesson I learned there, which over the years has proved more than beneficial. I quickly learned that tithing is important to God. It is scriptural. God blesses us when we give.

At the college we would meet every Wednesday morning for a short service. If I had money, I always put my small ten percent into the offering bag. It was never much, as I didn't have much. But God never failed to keep me supplied with everything I needed and I always had some money.

One cold winter day I was in my room. The college building was old, parts were still being renovated. It was a beautiful place, but it was cold. The heating system for such a large building was inadequate. I was curled up on my bed praying and trying to stay warm. I told God I was struggling with the cold. He knew of course, but I told no one else.

A few days later a large parcel arrived for me. I wasn't expecting anything. When I opened it, I found a warm cosy tracksuit, numerous pairs of socks and other items, plus to my surprise a tennis racket and some balls. In the grounds of the college there was a tennis court, and we all enjoyed a game. After a hard days study, it was good to get out in the fresh air and get some exercise.

Someone from my church had sent the parcel to me. I had told no one I was struggling with the cold. I knew my Heavenly Father had laid my need on someone's heart. I was thrilled and overawed by His goodness and grateful to the kind person who sent the parcel.

One of my fellow students noticed I always had a little money and had seen the arrival of my parcel. She was curious to know how I always had what I needed. I told her how I'd learned about tithing in church, and ever since it was something I always did and have continued to do. It's my way of showing Him my love and trust. You cannot out give God.

When I next saw her she beamed at me. "I've started to tithe, and you are right." She explained that she'd never had enough money and could hardly afford the things she needed. However, since she started giving to God from the little she had, her situation had changed dramatically. "God is blessing me," she said. "From now on I will always Tithe."

I was delighted and pleased to have been able to help her. Giving to God what is His, shows our faith and belief in Him. Some lessons are hard to learn, especially when they touch our pockets. But when we cast our bread upon the water, our Heavenly Father gives back so much more. We have to learn to trust Him. He knows our needs and in His mercy He supplies them.

Chapter 9

I left the college and returned home. For a couple of years life went on as normal. We were now attending the large Elim church closer to the centre of London. The minister Wynn Lewis was a great preacher and we learned a lot.

One Sunday morning, we saw the minister from our old church. Having been asked to leave by the elders, he also attended the Elim church. Fortunately, the congregation was so large, we seldom saw him. Even though his sin had caused pain and heartache, I was glad he had not turned away from God. I hoped in time healing and restoration could take place in his life. Nevertheless, I felt for his wife and children.

During our time in the Elim church, my sister's husband had taken on the role as head gardener in a private stately home, Arbury Hall situated in the small town of Nuneaton.

The three of us, but especially mother and me were keen to move away from London. It was no longer a fun place to be. One day mother was chatting on the phone to my sister and told her of our desire to leave London. She explained that finances made such a move nigh on impossible.

However, a few weeks later my sister rang with some exiting news. Apparently, there were two gate houses at the entrance to the estate, one of which was vacant. The owners of the Hall wanted tenants who could keep an eye on people going through the gate and to lock it at night.

My sister didn't know if we would be interested, as the building was small. She suggested we go up and have a look. To say we were keen was an understatement. Joseph wasn't bothered one way or the other. I prayed the property would be big enough for the three of us. Mother and I were happy at the thought of being close to my sister.

When the day came to go and view it, we were so excited. We arranged to meet my sister and her husband in a layby near the local hospital. The Hall was situated on the other side of the town.

I quite liked Nuneaton. It's famous for an

author called George Elliot. The small town was refreshing after the claustrophobic atmosphere of London. Not that we saw much of it as Fred drove through the town at quite a pace. I was driving and did my best to keep up. If I lost him we wouldn't know where to go.

When we arrived at the gate house, I instantly loved it, so did mother. It looked like something from a fairy tale. There were actually two gate houses with an archway between them. Locally they were known as the Round Towers, because they literally were small towers with normal cottage style buildings attached. Although from the road all you could see was the tower and a length of brick wall with no windows. However, once you drove through the archway you could see the wall was the back of the cottage.

The small building consisted of a bathroom, kitchen and small sitting room, all very cosy. There was a bedroom downstairs in the actual tower and one upstairs. However, at the top of the stairs there was a good sized landing, which we decided could be converted into a bedroom for me.

It was such a pretty cottage. Mother and I fell in love with it. I don't think Joseph was so keen, he liked living in London. However, mother had made up her mind. She was desperate to get out of London and in a way, so was I. She also wanted to be near my sister.

So it was decided we were moving to

Nuneaton and going to live in the gate house of Arbury Hall. It would be a squeeze, the property was small, and so it would mean serious decluttering. Most of our furniture would be way too big, but for me that added to the excitement. We were at the start of a new adventure.

The grounds of the hall were beautiful. From the main road you couldn't see it, but when you drove through the archway you were halted by a five barred gate, beyond which you could see the beautiful park, with acres of woodland, which my sister said we were allowed to walk in.

From the gate a narrow road led to Arbury Hall which opened to the public at holiday times. They also opened for different events like craft shows and open air concerts.

The house and estate are privately owned. The house itself is stunning, and famous for its beautiful ceilings. At the side of the house there's a large lake and beautiful gardens. It also has a tearoom and a small craft shop. For a few years I volunteered to work in the shop. I enjoyed it.

The requirement for living in the property was to be the gate keepers and security for the big house. Joseph took on the job. On the drive back to London all we could talk about was the cottage, we had so many plans.

The only negative was Joseph. He had nowhere to work … a man cave so to speak. He was a talented man and spent many hours in the attic of the flat building things. However, Margaret told us the estate manager was happy for him to put up a shed. This made a huge difference to Joseph's willingness to leave London. He also built a small shed for me to use as an art studio.

It was decided mother and I would remain in London until he had built the sheds. The poor man spent weeks sleeping rough in the cottage, working as fast as he could to get the sheds finished and complete the different jobs that needed doing in the cottage. Mother and I tried to be patient, but it was hard. We were packed and ready to move. Every thought, every conversation was the cottage.

We knew this move was a miracle, as financially there was no way we could afford to move. It was something we had prayed about and discussed for such a long time. Before my sister rang to tell us about the vacant cottage, we were resolved to staying in the flat. We had no other option. Or so we thought. However, God had other plans and on the day we drove to our new home we thanked and praised Him for His goodness and awesome provision.

* **

For the next few years' life carried on as it does. I spent a lot of time in the small studio Joseph had built for me, and overtime I amassed a quantity of art work. There were opportunities to exhibit, which I loved and surprisingly I made a little name for myself. There were also a few singing opportunities which I enjoyed.

I also did my best to help Emily the elderly lady living in the gatehouse across from us. I regularly did some shopping and cleaning for her. She was pretty much an invalid, being riddled with arthritis. She also had hugely swollen legs. She suffered with a lot of pain and had great difficulty walking or moving around. She was pretty much house bound. Although on occasion she would make her way slowly and painfully across to us for a coffee. We grew fond of her and did all we could to help.

The way things happen sometimes is truly miraculous. For a brief moment I would like to recount a story about Emily.

Like our cottage, Emely's tiny front room had thick walls and a deep window sill. It was covered with little ornaments. Once a week I would wash them for her, being careful not to break anything.

Among all the ornaments there was a pretty glass horse. It was coated with something that changed colour according to the weather. Emily always reminded me not to wash it, as she feared the coating would come off.

Being mad about horses, I was naturally attracted to this small ornament. It was so pretty and delicate. Emily, aware I liked it would smile and say.

'Who knows, one day it could be yours.' Although she warned me not to bank on it, as she knew her estranged family might not honour her wishes.

Sadly, one day when I returned with her shopping, I found Emily slumped in her chair, she had suffered a massive stroke. We called the doctor, and she was rushed into hospital. As predicted her family arrived, and a few days later she passed away.

As soon as the funeral was over, a large van appeared and they took everything. The small cottage was stripped bare. When they left I went over and peered in the window. It was so sad to see Emily's little home dark and empty. But to my amazement, left all alone on the windowsill was the little glass horse.

I rushed into the cottage and retrieved it. Tears streamed down my face as I thanked God, and my friend Emily for the gift of the little horse. It really was a miracle, as I know Emily had no contact with her family before she passed away, and while in the hospital she couldn't talk or move.

Now when I hold the glass horse I think of Emily, and the miraculous way God enabled me to receive what she wanted me to have. To me it's a testimony of how wonderful and thoughtful God is.

..
** **

Life was good in our new home. It was

certainly cosy, but we got on okay and on the whole we were happy. We had been living in the Round Tower a few years, when one day mother became ill. She was cold and no amount of blankets warmed her. Joseph and I knew it was serious. We called the Doctor and she was rushed into hospital.

She was in in there around seven weeks as they tried to find the cause of the problem. As a final test they did a spinal tap and at last got a result. She had a rare form of Leukaemia. Every few months her blood thickened, so she had to go to a clinic and have at least a pint removed.

For the rest of her life she took a cancer pill. She was seventy when first diagnosed. Thank the Lord; she remained in good health for another five years. Apart from regular hospital visits, mother remained well and life returned to normal.

At that time I knew very little about mother's condition. For some reason it didn't register that she had a rare form of cancer. The tablet she was taking was oral chemotherapy, so basically for those five years she was in remission.

It was during this time that mother began talking about my brother … wondering where he was and if he was okay. The last time we saw him was when we were living in London, it was just before we were to move to Nuneaton. As usual he turned up out of the blue, high on drugs. His eyes looked wild and he was limping. His unannounced appearances always made mother and me nervous.

This time he arrived in a particularly bad way ... angry and aggressive, especially to mother. I was forced to get between them and try to calm him down.

We were young Christians, and did our best to help him, but he wouldn't listen. All he did was rant about how wonderful Hitler was and how much he hated the Jews and wished they had been exterminated. His whole attitude was offensive, but we let it pass. It was useless to argue with him. I confess we breathed a sigh of relief when he left.

Having moved and made new lives we never heard from him again. Mother started to worry about him. After all, he was her son. She and I had long since renewed our mother and daughter relationship and I'm pleased to say we had grown close. All was forgiven and we had put the past behind us.

However, she'd had no opportunity to re-establish a relationship with Edward. The last time we saw him he left angry. I know the fact she had a terminal illness heightened mother's need to see him again.

I was aware the Salvation Army were good at finding missing people. I approached them and gave them all the details about him that I could. They took the case. I hoped it wouldn't take too long to find him, for mother's sake.

Chapter 10

We had found a good church and attended regularly. The congregation were friendly and caring. The preaching was excellent and most Sundays you could feel the power of God. We were always keen for Sunday to arrive. As soon as you walked into the building, there was an air of expectancy.

One Sunday, I met a lady that over the coming years I would be firm friends with. It had been a powerful meeting and I was overcome by the presence of the Lord. She approached me and said, "I want to tell you that Jesus loves you." It really blessed me. At the time we were new to the church and we didn't know many of the people there. The lady's name was Joy. She and her husband Bill had been with the church for a number of years. To this day they are my dear friends and have had a huge impact on my life.

Sadly, we had been in the Round Towers a couple of years, when my sister told us they were leaving. Fred had been offered the job as head gardener for a private estate in Buckinghamshire. We were sad they were going and we missed them. However, we had made a life for ourselves in Nuneaton and were happy.

We visited them on numerous occasions. Where they now lived was beautiful. The village was quaint and extremely pretty. In fact, the house they lived in and the village can be seen in a few episodes of Midsummer Murders on the television.

During this time, my sister gave us some worrying news. She'd been told that she had Multiple Sclerosis. We were shocked. It's a dreadful disease and we didn't know how to respond. Naturally, mother was devastated. Margaret was her baby girl. Thankfully, with my sister's type of MS, she would have a relapse and then for a while recuperate. The progression of the disease was slow. Not that that was much comfort. We kept in touch with them and visited frequently.

It was during one of their visit to us that mother was able to talk to Margaret without Fred being there. I can't remember where he was.

Nevertheless, mother had the wonderful privilege of leading my sister to the Lord. We had tried for so long to reach her. I knew she was interested. She would listen intently when we talked about the Lord and she happily accepted our prayers for the MS. So I was not wholly surprised when mother told me, my sister had accepted the Lord Jesus as her Saviour. This was awesome news. I was so happy for my sister and delighted for mother. What a privilege to lead your daughter to the Lord.

It wasn't easy for my sister, as Fred was quite hostile to all things religious, as he called it. Wisely, she kept what had happened to herself, which under the circumstances was probably the best thing. Fred didn't understand and made it clear, he wasn't interested. Nevertheless, it was good to be able to talk freely with my sister about the Lord. And I'm sure it helped her.

Life for us in Nuneaton went on as normal, we were happy and church was great. I had made a number of good friends, and enjoyed a varied social life. It was well known that I needed a job and as it turned out my friend Joy told me if I was interested the lady she worked for needed someone to do laundry work.

Joy had worked for this lady doing general cleaning for many years. She often said how much she enjoyed her job. She said the lady she worked for was lovely and she was sure I would like it. After thinking about it for a while, I accepted.

When I went for the interview I was amazed! The house was a mansion. Two houses could have been built in the lounge alone. It was beautiful. In the basement there was a swimming pool, its size the same footprint as the lounge.

My interview went well and I got the job. I started in October 1992. It turned out to be the best decision I ever made. My new employer was a nice lady. She and her husband had three school age children and two dogs. It was a happy place to work.

Over the years I grew extremely fond of her and remained in her employ for over twenty years. Life was good. I was happy at work and attended a thriving church and considering mother's condition she too was doing well.

I had joined a local art group and enjoyed it. On occasion we had a visiting artist who would demonstrate and teach us new techniques and mediums to work in. We held regular exhibitions. A major one was held each year during March in the local museum and art gallery.

One evening we went as a group to a studio not far from town and watched two sculptors, John Letts and Keith Lee, working. They were well known, both having their work exhibited in the town. A life size statue of the famous author George Elliot sculpted by John and aided by Keith, is on permanent display in the town centre. She lived and worked in Nuneaton.

John Letts had a bust of the Queen in the

foyer of the local hospital. Keith Lee had work displayed in the hospice close by. They were both nice and extremely talented. It was a brilliant evening. We got to try our hands at moulding some clay and enjoyed a cup of tea and an interesting talk by John.

During the evening, I found myself sitting beside Keith. We had a good chat and I must confess I found him fascinating, in more ways than one. As I've previously stated I've never bothered about men and never wanted a serious relationship. However, I confess to stirrings of interest in this man and I felt he liked me. Unbeknown to me seeds were being planted. I now know God was preparing me for a huge change in my life.

I didn't see much of Keith after that. Occasionally, our paths would cross at a local craft fair, but nothing more. Whenever, we met I must admit, my liking for him grew and I found myself thinking about him.

One evening in December 1993, I was in church. We had a visiting minister from Ireland, Barry White. In the evening service I went up for prayer. Over the past few days I had felt tired and heady. He prayed for me, I felt better and returned to my seat. I had my eyes closed as we sang, 'I love You Lord,' I felt someone standing beside me. I opened my eyes, it was the minister. He asked what was wrong with me. I told him I was tired. He said it was caused by emotion and hurt.

Quietly, I told him about my childhood. He prayed for me. As he prayed I slipped onto my chair and wept as God dealt with me. Afterwards he knelt beside me and asked if I was married and how old I was. He told me, all was forgiven and forgotten.

After the service I went and thanked him. He asked me a few more questions. I shared the bad experience I'd had at Bible College. He said he already knew. God had told him. He said I must let it go. God had forgiven me.

He told me not to bottle things up, to be open. A man was coming into my life and the end will be better than the beginning. He said God loves me and that I am a lovely woman of God. He asked to be invited to the wedding. I laughed, but must admit to being taken aback. Marriage had never been on the cards as far as I was concerned. Being abandoned by my parents as well as my stepfather, I found it hard to consider the idea of marriage and I had never wanted children, and by now I was too old anyway.

The thought of marriage and surrendering to a man freaked me out. I felt they couldn't be trusted. How could I be sure I wouldn't be abandoned and rejected?

At this point, I hasten to add. I had long since forgiven my birth father and my stepfather. Nevertheless, I wasn't sure I could love a man. So much hurt had hardened my heart.

However, I hadn't taken into account the love

of Jesus. He was a man and I adored Him. I had surrendered to Him wholeheartedly. So I had to believe that with God all things are possible. If He wanted me to marry, He would have to help me. But my goodness, the man would have to be someone special. I know now, God is the best match maker.

As I digested what the minister had said, he went on to say that I will love passionately, but not in a sexual way. He stressed again, that I am loved. He asked to pray for me again with one of our ministers. They prayed for release in my emotions. It was an amazing and wonderful evening. I went home buzzing. The thought, I am accepted in the beloved, gave me such a sense of peace. I felt as though this was the beginning of the rest of my life. I had come out of the shadows. I knew God loved me and would always look after me. But having it spoken over my life by a stranger, filled me with such joy and peace.

When I got home, I wrote down what he'd said while it was fresh in my mind. I'm glad I did. Reading it again after all these years and being able to add it to my story is a real blessing.

*** ***

Time past and I grew restless for a place of my own. It was okay living with mother and Joseph, but I needed my own space ... my own home. Mother understood. It took a while and I struggled to be patient, but eventually in late 1993 the estate informed me there was a cottage available to rent, if I was interested. It was in the tiny hamlet of Astley next door to the studios of John Letts and Keith Lee the man I met when I went with the art group.

It was the sweetest semi-detached cottage, a one up and one down. The lounge was cosy and next to that was a tiny basic kitchen. Upstairs, next to the bedroom was a surprisingly modern shower room. The place was quaint and old fashioned. I instantly fell in love with it. The couple living next door were extremely friendly. Living out in the country it was nice to know they were there.

It was as well I had my little car. Otherwise I would have struggled to get to work, go into town, or see mother and Joseph. I also had a bicycle. I loved riding round the country lanes. I had been told there was a small shed attached to the cottage. I decided it would be a good place to store my bike.

However, when I opened it, the small space was full of moulds belonging to the sculptors next door. There was only one thing for it, I had to go and ask them to move the moulds. One morning after breakfast I walked into the studious. The smell of resin hit me, it was so strong. I wondered how they could both work in it and John Letts smoked which added to the overpowering smell.

When I walked in they were taking a break.

John stood by a desk drinking a coffee. Keith sat in a chair by the wall. I had my back to Keith as I asked John about the moulds. In my periphery vison I could see Keith watching me. I noticed John smile slightly.

Feeling Keith's eyes on me I turned and smiled. I was offered a coffee which I accepted. I stayed about an hour chatting with them. I must admit, I felt a stirring of interest while talking with Keith. Even in his mucky work clothes I found him extremely attractive. I had a feeling he felt the same about me.

For the first few months it was a tentative getting to know each other. I would find any excuse to go into the studio and watch them work. On Saturday mornings Keith would open the studio, in case customers popped in. They had a large loyal following from right around the country and abroad. It was easier for Keith to do it as he lived in Nuneaton, while John and his wife Pat lived a few miles away.

We would have a coffee together and talk. I was delighted when I found out he was a Christian, as were John and Pat. So our discussions more often than not, were theological. At the time he was studying the Old Testament, especially the Jewish temple. He made it sound fascinating.

Down the road from us, the farm shop had set up a tearoom and bakery in an old barn. It was lovely. In the winter there was a roaring log fire. I would meet friends there. We would cluster round the fire with our fresh crusty rolls or cream cakes. I always kept an eye on the door hoping Keith would come in for cakes, most days he did. If my timing was right I would see him and we would have a quick chat before he went back to work.

One evening there was a knock on my cottage door, it was Keith. He had accidently locked the studio door and left his car keys inside. He needed a lift home to get the spare keys. As you can imagine I was delighted to offer him a lift. He lived in a nice part of the town. His detached house was in a small pleasant coppice with just a few other houses. I waited in the car while he ran in and got the spare car key, and then I drove him back to the studio. I was delighted to have been able to help him.

There's a day I will always remember. Once a year he used to drive to a beautiful village in Wales called Betws-y-coed and this time I was going with him. A large craft shop in the village sold his and John's sculptures. When I arrived at the studio they had loaded crates of sculptures in the back of the car. Some of the work was solid bronze. I was surprised the cars suspension didn't collapse under the weight.

The journey went well and the weather was lovely. We chatted all the way, sharing our lives and getting to know each other. When we arrived at the village we went straight to the craft shop. Keith helped them store the sculptures and accepted payment.

Leaving the shop we had a gentle stroll round the village heading in the direction of a quaint café. On the way we walked by the river it was lovely. The village buzzed with enthusiastic hikers enjoying the facilities and the challenging walks. To me, some of the surrounding hills looked more like mountains. It really was a beautiful place.

After a welcome cup of coffee we decided to drive further on and spend some time by the sea. It was a great day, culminating in dinner back in Betws-y-coed, before the long drive home.

That night I lay in my bed, my thoughts full of Keith and the wonderful day we had spent together. I knew I was falling for him. As I lay there I recalled what a friend had told me. She said she'd had a dream about a man who was coming into my life. She said he had blue eyes and dark hair and was wearing a shiny grey suit. She said in the dream he looked really nice.

I later saw Keith wearing a shiny grey suit. He wore it when he came to support me in the ministry I was doing at the time. I used my artwork and combined it with singing. My friend saw him and confirmed he was the man in her dream. I was so excited. It was only in the past couple of years I had started thinking about having a man in my life. Up until then I was content being single. But Barry White's prophecy and my friend's dream encouraged me to accept the idea that God had a plan for my life, and it included a man and it would seem that man was Keith.

Chapter 11

Not long after Keith and I started to see each other, Joseph went into hospital. He was seriously ill. He asked if Keith would go and see him, which he did. Joseph had been a professing Christian as long as I had known him. But he struggled and lapsed many times. His greatest weakness was smoking. He tried often to give it up, but didn't succeed. He would spend hours in his shed with the doors and windows closed smoking non-stop.

In my studio next door, I painted with oils and even with the strong smell of turps I could smell the cigarettes. So I dread to think what condition his lungs were in. I guess the fact he went into hospital hardly able to breathe and was put on continued oxygen says it all.

When Keith saw him at the hospital he was in a bad way. Keith told us Joseph grabbed his hand and begged him to lead him in the sinner's prayer. Keith did and also prayed for him. Joseph died shortly after. The funeral was small, mainly mother, myself, Keith and Joseph's daughter and her partner. They came over from Holland.

After Joseph died, mother could no longer afford to live in the Round Towers. But not only that, she didn't like being on her own. Plus, the estate needed someone with authority to keep a check on the gate. It was a man's job. Now mother was alone they pushed for her to leave.

Thank God we found a nice flat for her in a block for elderly people. A warden lived in the block and checked on the residence every morning, which gave mother and us some sense of security. Apart from her new home being a first floor flat with steep stairs, it was perfect, and she was happy and soon settled in.

I think my fledging relationship with Keith added to her happiness. She knew her illness was serious and the thought I had found someone I liked, pleased her. She had begun to worry about what would happen to me when she was gone. I liked the fact she had motherly concerns for me, but on the negative side, I spent a lot time convincing her I was more than capable of taking care of myself, whether I married or not.

When I first introduced her to Keith, she loved him. However, when we were alone she shared her concern that he was ten years older than me. I knew she was relating it to her own situation and the loss of my stepfather, who was sixteen years older than mother. I know she still grieved for him.

She was concerned that at some point the age difference, though unimportant now, in later years could become a problem. She didn't want me to find myself in her situation. Even though she liked Keith, she did her best to make sure, I was sure.

Considering I had never wanted marriage or children, I was surer about my feelings for Keith than I was about many other things in my life. I knew deep down God had brought him into my life. And there is no better match maker than God.

We both had our issues, baggage if you like that we brought into the relationship. I guess that's normal for most couples. I still struggled a bit with insecurity, relationship issues and fear of rejection. With God's help I was so much better, but occasionally my fears from the past would rear their ugly heads.

Keith had come out of a broken marriage. His wife had left him for another man, taking their son with her. However, they remained friends, which I think is a credit to them both. After he had proposed to me, he arranged a meal in a restaurant. To which he invited John and Pat and his ex-wife. I must admit, initially, I was nervous of meeting her, but John and Pat knew her well and reassured me. They were right. She was happy for Keith … for both of us. I liked her and it turned out to be a pleasant evening.

* *
** **

To use an old fashioned word, Keith and I courted for six months. I was over the moon when he asked me to marry him. Of course my answer was yes. He took me into town and we chose a lovely diamond engagement ring, which I proudly showed to everyone. My employer and my dear friend Joy were so pleased for me. I know Joy was relieved. She would no longer have to convince me of Keith's affection for me. The poor woman never knew what to expect when I picked up for work in the mornings. It was a case of. Does he love me, does he not? I was so insecure. We laugh about it now.

Once we were engaged, and had set a date, I was so happy. I found it hard to believe that at the age of forty eight I was going to be married. So much had happened in my life much of it negative. Nevertheless, I had no time to dwell on memories from my past or insecure thoughts. The fact Keith had asked me to marry him, was proof enough of his feelings for me, no matter my age.

The lovely lady I worked for offered me her own wedding dress. I was delighted to accept. It was beautiful. The long sleeved top was covered with embroidered lace. The long skirt was a soft floaty material over a silk underskirt. She was extremely good at baking and made a gorgeous three tiered wedding cake for us. She also offered us her holiday house in Devon for our honeymoon. I was truly grateful.

Keith and I found a place locally for our reception. Joy organized all the food as a wedding gift and her husband Bill offered to give me away. He often jokes. He had to give me away as Keith wouldn't pay. Over the many years I've known them, they've always made me feel like I was part of the family. They did the same for Keith. They have and always will have a special place in my heart.

Another couple I love dearly are David and Ruth. Joy and Bill first introduced me to them. I took to Ruth right away. She's a lovely lady in all ways. She has a great sense of humour. We have been close friends from the first day we met. Both Keith and I love spending time with them. We always have fun. I particularly love to discuss spiritual matters with David. We don't always agree, but it's certainly challenging and informative. He's a great preacher … a man of God who truly knows the word.

David ministers in a village church not far from Nuneaton. He also preaches in different churches around this part of the country and occasionally abroad. We look upon David as our pastor. David and Ruth are two people we trust completely and go to for spiritual help and advice.

Once a week Ruth and I go out for a coffee with another friend we both love, Paula. I first met her when she came to the church Keith and I started in Grendon. We bonded instantly. She has such a gentle spirit. Her life has been intertwined with ours for many years now. Keith and I love her dearly.

Keith and I hoped that David would be free to officiate at our wedding. To our delight he was free. I would not have wanted anyone else to marry us. Because I knew with David, the gospel would be preached and it was.

And so on the 30th of September 1995 Keith and I were married. Though I say it myself, it was a beautiful wedding. It was such a blessing to have my mother and my sister and her family there. Mother read, 1 Corinthians 13 for us.

Towards the end of the service I held Keith's hands and sang 'One Hand, One Heart,' from West Side story. I wasn't sure emotionally if I would be able to do it, but thank the Lord I did. I know it blessed Keith and from what I was told, it blessed the congregation.

We were fortunate that a kind friend videoed the ceremony and reception for us. When we returned from our honeymoon in Devon, he gave us the video. He had done a brilliant job editing it and adding background music. It was lovely to be able to watch it ... to be reminded of a wonderful and happy day.

Initially, it felt strange moving from my tiny cottage into Keith's large detached house, but I soon settled in. I wouldn't dream of telling you that everything was perfect. We were happy together, but naturally we had our ups and downs, after all we were strangers. We had only known each other for six months before marrying, so it was a huge learning curve for us both.

I think maybe it was a little harder for me. Over the years I had become extremely independent. I had to, as there was no support from my family. As I've already shared, for many years we were estranged.

Due to my upbringing, it had been a case of go out into the world and survive or go under. No way was I going under. Until the day I got saved, I had always been self-sufficient ... a street wise survivor.

On our return from honeymoon, life took on some semblance of normality. Keith went back to work with John and I returned to my cleaning job. Most weekends Keith and I would load up our caravan with boxes of sculptures and go to different craft shows around the country. John and Pat did the same but they went to different venues.

I enjoyed it. I liked meeting the different craft folk, they were a nice crowd. We didn't make a lot of money. Keith had more people turn up at our stall for prayer than to buy something. Nevertheless, I enjoyed it, especially in the evening when we all returned to our caravans and had a barbecue. The aroma of the different foods being cooked floated over the camp site. It must have driven the local foxes mad.

For a year or so this was our lives, until Keith decided it was time to retire. In some ways I wasn't sorry. I found it tiring traveling to the different shows, unloading and then reloading heavy boxes filled with bronze sculptures and then on Monday morning having to go back to work.

It was 1999 and not long after Keith retired, a traumatic situation arose for my employer, and she needed someone to come and live in the house with her, as the property was huge. She mentioned it while we were having our morning coffee. I felt a nudge from the Lord that this was something Keith and I should do. I told her I was interested, but naturally I needed to discuss it with Keith. We talked it over and decided it would be a good idea.

When I told my employer she was delighted, a month or so later our house was rented out and we moved into a small self-contained apartment upstairs in my employer's house. On the whole it worked well for all concerned. Keith took on the role of house security and I continued with my own work. There was room for me to continue with my painting and Keith had a small office. So we were well catered for.

Obviously, there were pros and cons as there is nowhere like your own home. Nevertheless, we remained there for five years, and were reasonably happy. During that time Keith and I continued to run our small church in Gredon. Our congregation was small but dedicated. We had some wonderful times with the Lord and some life changing experiences. Some in the congregation found their gifting, including me.

While living in my employer's home, I found a new interest. Not something I ever imagined I would enjoy. It started because a friend at our church had bought three pet rats for her children. They had booked to go on holiday and asked if I would look after them. Being terrified of rats I wasn't at all keen, but my friend was desperate. So grudgingly I said yes. Even though she told me they were friendly and playful, I wasn't convinced.

When they arrived, I took a deep breath and looked in the cage. I don't know what I imagined. I suppose a large brown creature with beady eyes and sharp teeth. However, these were really quite pretty. They were different colours. I remember one was an attractive gold colour and they were smaller than I expected.

My employer's handyman made a barrier out of hard board for me, so the rats could have free run on the landing, as my friend said they won't want to be stuck in their cage for the two weeks they were away. She kept reassuring me they were friendly and would want to play with me. Unconvinced, I frowned at her, all she did was laugh.

However, as evening came they started to take an interest in their surroundings. Every time I walked past the cage they would come up to the bars and stare at me. I started to feel guilty. So Keith helped me put up the wooden barrier and we checked all the doors were closed. Then he went into the lounge and left me to deal with them. My hands trembled as I opened the cage door and stood back. In my mind I was thinking, I dare not touch them, so how will I get them back in cage.

Moving away from the cage I sat on the floor and prayed they wouldn't notice me, but once they finished investigating the area around their cage, they made a beeline for me. I was tempted to scream for Keith but as they approached and sniffed me, I calmed down. They climbed on me and played with my hair, I even got what I suppose you could call ratty kisses. I admit it wasn't long before I was enjoying them and laughing at their antics.

Hearing the laughter, Keith came to investigate. The moment he appeared, they ran down the hall to greet him. He wasn't scared like me and let them climb up his trousers. Grinning, he walked towards me. They followed him, swarming excitedly around his feet. It reminded me of the story of the Pied Piper of Hamlin.

From that night on I was smitten and decided I must have some of my own. Having them for that fortnight was such fun and I quickly realised they enjoyed human company and unlike hamsters, they didn't bite.

When my friend returned from her holiday and came to take them home, I missed them so much. I couldn't wait to go to the pet shop and buy one for myself. I chose a pretty brown and white boy, actually, he chose me. When I put my hand in the cage, which was full of squirming baby rats, he was the one who climbed up my arm and settled on my shoulder.

I bought a cage and everything he needed and proudly took him home. In no time, both Keith and I were smitten, he was so small, cute and friendly we both fell in love with him. Mind you, he soon grew into a big cuddly boy. I named him Coco. He was the beginning of my foray into breeding and showing. At which I did quite well. My employer was good about it and didn't seem to mind too much.

Chapter 12

We had been with my employer for a few years and had settled into a comfortable routine. In the early days I had wondered if the arrangement would work, as a live-in job can sometimes be difficult. Those living in can feel their freedom is compromised. While the person they are living with and working for, can feel a loss of privacy. However, this was not so in our case. On the whole, the situation worked well. We each of us were careful not to encroach on the others space, as much as possible anyway.

It was surprising how quickly the years flew by. It was early in 2002 and life took a sudden sad turn. My mother began to struggle with her illness and started spending more and more time in hospital. Her hair began to thin and fall out. We realised that was due to the cancer tablet Hydroxyurea. She had taken it for the past five years.

Life was hard for her. She struggled to eat and had lost weight ... a lot of weight! She looked like a walking skeleton, but with a huge swollen stomach. The swelling was her spleen.

She was so weak she hadn't the strength to have a bath. She asked me if I would help her. Naturally, I said yes, but I admit, the thought of helping her bathe made me feel a little embarrassed. However, the first time I helped her, she was so grateful and desperate for a warm bath, that all embarrassment disappeared. I felt privileged to assist her.

When I think about my young days and the lack of relationship with my mother, it amazed me that now I was helping her in a profoundly personal way. Only God can make such things possible. If we let Him, He can mend a broken relationship and heal all the hurt. Nothing is too hard for Him.

The first time I helped her bathe, I was shocked by how thin she was. There was absolutely no flesh on her. Her skin hung in loose folds. Having only seen her dressed, I hadn't realised how much weight she had lost, or how huge the spleen had become.

Mother didn't remain at home for long. She

slowly deteriorated and ended up back in hospital. In the middle of May mother had an operation to remove her spleen. We were not sure of the outcome, neither was the surgeon, she was so poorly he warned us she might not survive. We braced ourselves for the worst outcome. I say worst, but in a way it would have been better if she had died during the operation. She was a Christian, so we knew she was safe with God. All we could do was pray God's will into the situation.

However, she came through and when we saw the surgeon a few days later, his callous comment upset me. In a dismissive way, he told us he'd doubted she would make it. When she did, he called her, 'A tough old bird.' At the time my attention was focused on mother, so I ignored his heartless comment, but I've never forgotten it.

When I saw her after the operation, with all the tubes and wires attached. I saw how brave she was, and I remembered his comment, it made me angry. She was tough, in a positive way. But with all she had to go through in the coming weeks, I often think, perhaps it would have been better for her if she had not survived the operation.

But these are not decisions for us to make, it's up to God. He has the final word. Even though to us everything looks like a disaster, His timing is always right, and we have to trust Him. Not always easy when a loved one is suffering.

Mother never truly recovered and slowly

went downhill. She wouldn't eat, so the nurses put a tube down her nose into her stomach, so they could give her liquid food. Initially, mother refused to let them do it. But I was there at the time and encouraged her to have it done. Naively, I thought if she can get some nourishment inside her, she will gain strength and be able to go home. It didn't work and she continued to deteriorate.

In many ways, I feel bad about the whole situation. In the five years since she was first diagnosed, for some reason it didn't sink in that my mother had cancer … a rare form of leukaemia. She took her tablets, went to her clinical reviews and had her blood which regularly thickened, removed. We would sit with a nurse for a good half hour waiting for the blood to fill the bag.

The clinic where this took place was cramped, dark and oppressive. So often it seemed we had to wait ages for the treatment and to see her oncologist. When there were more than five patients in the waiting room it was claustrophobic. None of us enjoyed it, least of all my brave mother.

In hindsight, when I think about the way her life ended, it makes me sad and in way I feel guilty. She had no real medical support, and towards the end I feel I should have done more, at least tried to get her into a hospice. If I had, her last days before passing would have been more comfortable.

The hospital did their best, but as normal there was a bed shortage and they made us feel she was bed blocking. Seeing as she was in there from early May until the day she died on the 20th July, I suppose she was. Towards the end she was on Morphine and her passing was peaceful. We were all with her, me, my sister and Keith. It was sad for us, but I was pleased for mother. Now she was with the Lord. She was safe and in no more pain.

After her cremation on the 29th July, mother's flat had to be completely cleared; all carpets and curtains had to be removed along with furniture and personal items. Joseph's daughter and partner came over from Holland with their van and helped us. We were so grateful. We could never have done it without them. There was a time limit in which to clear the place. It took about two days of non-stop work to do it and by the end we were all exhausted.

Fortunately, after living with my employer for five years, Keith and I had decided it was time to return to our own home. The estate agent who organised the letting for us, informed the tenant it was time to leave.

It worked out well, as quite a few of my mother's possessions like her fridge, some of her furniture and the carpets and curtains were useful for our own home. Joseph's daughter and partner loaded their van and took the stuff to our house. We had to make a few trips and by the time we had finished we were shattered. Not just because of the work, but the emotional impact. Seeing mother's home stripped bare and knowing she was gone, was hard.

For a while I felt like an orphan. My birth father, my stepfather and Joseph were all gone, and now my mother. It was just me, my sister and Keith. I thanked the Lord for Keith. It made me realise even more how God knows the beginning from the end and makes provision for His children.

When I reflect on that time and mothers passing, I'm grateful God made the way for us to heal what had once been a tense and fractured relationship.

* *
** **

Keith and I didn't leave my employer right away. She needed time to find a replacement for us. Not only that, our house needed a lot of refurbishment. We decided to have a conservatory built on the back of the house. The kitchen and bathroom needed redoing and everywhere needed decorating. By the time everything we wanted was done, the house looked wonderful and we couldn't wait to move back in.

While we were busy preparing to return home, I received a letter from the Salvation Army. It was about my brother Edward. Apparently, he was found by a man lying on the pavement in Islington, a suburb of London. The kind man got him into the local hospital where my brother died. His death was drug related. Which came as no surprise, nevertheless I was sad ... such a waste of a young life.

He died in 1999, but I didn't receive the letter until late July 2002. The Salvation Army had to be sure this person was my brother. Going by the full name, date of birth and other details, everything appeared to be correct. It upset me to think of his sad end. When I told my sister Margaret she was devastated. We were both grateful mother would never have to know.

I received the letter a week after mother's death. Had it arrived before, I would have felt obligated to tell her. She would never have coped with such news. He was her only son and I know she would have blamed herself for the way he turned out.

I know we make our own choices in life. Nevertheless, I believe upbringing and parental relationships play a huge part in how a child thrives and copes with the world. Hearing such news she would have been devastated and guilt ridden. I know the reason she wanted him found was to make amends. So you can imagine my relief. She would never know. Again I have to say God's timing is perfect. He is so wonderful and gracious.

* *
** **

153

Finally, in May 2003, we returned to our own home. I still continued working for my employer, but my days had been cut down to two. Another couple were now living with her, which I was pleased about. We didn't want her to be on her own. They were nice people. She had known them for quite some time. They were old friends, so it had all worked out rather well.

Keith and I were looking forward to our first Christmas since returning home. We had invited my sister and her family to spend the day with us. Unfortunately, a couple of days before Christmas I started to have a lot of pain in the back of my left leg.

I had no idea what was wrong. Taking pain killers enabled me to keep going. But on Christmas Eve the pain had become excruciating so I went to the Doctor. He examined me and because I had no feeling in my foot he became concerned and ordered an ambulance to take me to the Walsgrave hospital in Coventry, where he had arranged for a scan.

I tried to tell him I had family arriving on Christmas day and I didn't have time to go the hospital, but he was insistent. He said the ambulance would pick me up from my house.

I was only home a short while before the ambulance arrived and whisked me off to the hospital. I didn't protest too much as I really was suffering.

The only time I was comfortable and out of

pain was during the scan as I had a large pillow under my knees and for some reason that eased my discomfort. I didn't like the scan though. I found it claustrophobic and noisy. Once it was over, I was taken up to a ward to await the results. I sat on the bed trying not to panic. This was our first Christmas back home and no way did I want to miss it. I was looking forward to spending some time with my sister and her family.

I prayed the results would be positive and thank God when the Doctor arrived he came with good news. There was nothing wrong as far as my spine went, but what was causing the pain he had no idea, neither did I. I just wanted to get out of there and go home.

A nurse took me to a quiet waiting area where I rang Keith. The poor man had been out and when he got home he wondered where I was. I told him not to worry and just come and pick me up. I was trying not to panic. There was so much to do in preparation for the next day.

Between the two of us we prepared what food we could in advance. I hobbled around laying the table and making sure everything was as ready as possible. By the time I'd finished, our new conservatory looked gorgeous. The Christmas tree stood in the corner ... fairy lights twinkling. The dining table looked wonderfully festive. As much as possible, we were ready. Had it not been for my painful leg and the stressful day in the hospital, I would have been happier.

Christmas morning, we were up early finishing things off. When my sister and the family arrived I managed to hide my discomfort and we all had a lovely time. Under the circumstances our Christmas lunch was excellent. My sister and her husband Fred were never ones for staying anywhere too long and by the time we finished our after dinner coffee, they were ready to go home.

I'll be honest, I wasn't sorry. My leg hurt and I felt unwell. We said our goodbyes and I went upstairs to put something comfy on. All I wanted to do was lie on the couch and rest.

As I changed my clothes, I heard Keith's sharp intake of breath. I'll always remember his words. "My goodness, I think you have Shingles. There's a rash all the way down the back of your leg." I know it sounds weird, but in a way I was relieved. It's horrible and frustrating not knowing what's causing such pain.

Needless to say we drove to the emergency surgery at our local hospital. Long story short, I did indeed have Shingles. Keith drove me home and then took the prescription for antivirals to a chemist which was fortunately open.

With all that had happened in the past few months, the death of my mother and the sad news about my brother Edward, as well as the stress of moving back home. I guess it was hardly surprising I had Shingles. It had been a sad and traumatic time.

I was grateful to have Keith. He certainly is God's gift to me. Don't get me wrong, we have our ups and downs. We may be Christians, but there are occasions when there are disagreements and things can get heated! The secret I believe to a good marriage is praying together and always being quick to say, "I'm sorry."

Strengthened by my faith in God and with Keith by my side, I have been able to face most of what life throws at me. But there would be a few situations to come, that would truly test my faith.

Chapter 13

In the beginning of 2004, life carried on as normal. I was kept busy with work and looking after my numerous pet rats. Keith was occupied with the work of our church. We all looked forward to Sunday evenings. There was always an air of excitement. We never knew what God would say to us. I was privileged to choose the music and lead the worship. We ran the church for nearly fifteen years. It was a blessed time. During many of the services I and others in the congregation were mightily used by God. It's a time I will never forget, I miss it terribly. In those fifteen years I grew in spiritual confidence.

I believe we all did.

But one Sunday during the service I felt God's presence and it was as though He said, "Let go of that which you are holding onto so tightly." There was more, but I can no longer remember it. The word was confirmed by another lady in the congregation. We none of us had any idea what God was trying to tell us. However, on the following Thursday, Keith received a letter telling him that the church council wanted the building back as the land had been sold to a developer.

It was a sad way to end after all those years, and for a while Keith and I felt lost and unhappy. We had to lay our ministries aside and trust God for whatever future He had planned for us. It was hard and yet at the same time we were grateful for God's warning. It softened the blow and knowing He was with us was a comfort.

Our God knows all things and sometimes He asks us to lay down something precious, whatever it may be and trust Him. I have learned that life consists of seasons. Each one is a time of spiritual growth and should be embraced not feared. Even when a new season brings pain and distress, we never walk the new path alone. He has promised He will never leave us, or forsake us and in my own life I know that to be true.

The site of our church is now a small housing estate. We prayed all the new houses would know the peace that we experienced as we worshiped God in that community hall.

After a few weeks of prayer and seeking guidance, we returned to the church in which we were married. But I have to confess nowhere has come close to what we experienced in that small hall in Grendon.

** **

Later that year in August, my sister Margaret told us she and Fred were moving to live in Southern Ireland. It was all rather hurried. We found out later that they left their employment under a cloud. We never truly found out what was going on. Suffice to say there were accusations and Fred was fired.

He had been the head gardener on the estate for a quite a few years, so the news came as a shock. More so for them I imagine. Not long after my sister told us, they were gone. It all happened so fast. Again, I was glad our mother was not alive. I know Margaret leaving and going to live so far away would have upset her.

There were a number of sad events in 2004. In November of that year, Pat the wife of Keith's partner John lets, passed away. She had bravely fought cancer. John told us she died peacefully in his arms.

I felt for Keith. He had known John and Pat

for many years and was extremely fond of them. In fact after Keith and his wife split up, he had lived with John and Pat for a number of years. They looked upon him as family, as he did them. Pat's passing affected Keith deeply and John was never the same. He had always been outgoing, but he became quiet and withdrawn. It was a sad time.

In December, I too received sad news. My dear friend Sadie had died of cancer. I knew she was poorly. We had regularly kept in touch by phone and with occasional visits. Originally, she had breast cancer, which she had come through successfully.

After her treatment for breast cancer, she recovered and was doing well, but tragically something awful happened that changed everything. She rang me late one evening. I could tell she was in a terrible state. Through her tears she told me her eldest son Matthew, who was my godson, was dead.

He was spending the weekend at his friend's house. They had a boating lake and the young men decided to row out into the middle of the lake and look at the stars. When they rowed back to the jetty and climbed out of the boat, Matthew fell into the water. They couldn't rescue him. He was wearing heavy winter cloths and drowned.

I couldn't believe what she was telling me. It was horrendous ... unreal. Sadly, we were unable to go to his funeral. In a way I was glad, because to be honest I didn't know how I would cope. I loved Matthew. He was a real character. It was hard to believe that at such a young age, he had died.

Sadie never recovered from the shock, and when she rang and told me the cancer had returned, I was devastated for her. The cancer affected her liver and her battle with the disease was short.

We went to London to see her and when I walked into the house, I had to hide my shock. The person standing in the room with yellow skin and bloated face was not my beautiful friend. But then physical beauty is only skin deep. Sadie radiated a spiritual beauty. She had always been a gentle person and even now with all she had suffered, there was a quiet peace and serenity about her.

I hope I hid my shock from her, it wasn't easy. It was hard for Keith as well. One crumb of comfort was the fact that her daughter in law, who was married to her younger son Adam, was pregnant. She would have a grandchild. Keith and I prayed she would live to see the baby.

However, not long after our visit, we received the news from her husband that she had passed away. Her funeral in early December 2004 was sad but beautiful. She was a special lady and much loved by everyone who knew her. I am so glad she died a Christian. I know I will see her again.

* *
** **

In Jan 2005 my sister rang to say they would be returning to the UK. Ireland was too expensive and with my sister having MS it was no doubt doubly hard for them as there is no NHS in Southern Ireland. She said they would be returning sometime in the spring. I was delighted and couldn't wait for them to come. However, things took a tragic and shocking turn. Even now, thinking about it, is upsetting.

March the 9th 2005 was a normal day, until my mobile phone rang. Thank the Lord Keith answered it. I could hear what he was saying, but I couldn't understand the gist of the conversation. He was saying something about an accident and both dead.

We knew Fred was taking HGV lessons, so I assumed they had crashed, or something. I could feel panic rising and started to dial my sister's number on the landline. There was no answer. All the while Keith was on the phone, I tried to ask him what was going on. Even listening to half a conversation, I knew it was bad.

When the call ended, Keith told me he had been talking to the Garda, the Irish police. He made me sit down. I kept asking him, "What's wrong?" I could see he was shaken up and didn't know how to tell me. Even now, all these years later I feel emotional thinking about it.

Keith said the police were called to a fire at my sister's home. The property was completely destroyed. The fire had been so intense it burned through the ground as well as the building. From the forensics they told us, it would seem that Fred shot my sister as she slept. He then shot the two dogs, doused the house with fuel, set it alight and shot himself.

In the intensity of the fire nothing survived. My sister Margaret and Fred were burned beyond recognition, even their teeth. There was nothing to tell the police who they were. Amazingly, the police found my sister's phone it had melted in the intense heat. But miraculously, they were able to retrieve one number from the burned sim card, it was mine, hence the distressing phone call. Nevertheless, I am so grateful to God for that miracle.

Every detail of this awful incident is fresh in my mind and always will be. It's like a horror film that plays over and over again. At the time I was numb, I couldn't cry, I couldn't think. I told myself it wasn't real, it didn't happen.

At work I went through the motions. It was such a shocking thing, all those around us, friends, and church family didn't know what to say, or how to respond. It was a hard and distressing time. Especially when we found out that Fred did it because of dept. They owed thousands, but he was too proud to seek help.

Keith and my nephew Ben, Margaret's son went over to Ireland. The police wanted to speak to them. It seems they were concerned there might be an IRA connection. There wasn't of course. But poor

Keith and Ben underwent a long interrogation by the Irish police.

I felt for my nephew. I couldn't begin to imagine how he felt. I was traumatised by it. How much worse it must have been for him. He was a young man who had lost his parents in a horrendous way. Sometimes, an awful thought goes through my mind. I think what if Ben had been with them. Knowing Fred as I did. I believe Ben would have died too. It doesn't bare thinking about.

I am so grateful to God that my beautiful nephew, my sister's son is safe and living happily with his lovely partner and family. I'm sure at times he must struggles with the awful memory of it. I know I do. It's good that when we are with them, we are able to talk freely about it.

The funeral took place in Ireland. We didn't go. I'll be honest, I couldn't face it. I wanted to remember my sister as she was. I didn't want to see the coffins and know that basically they were both empty, as the bodies were so badly burned. I wanted to keep my lovely baby sister alive in my memory. I miss her and think about her often.

A memorial service was held for them in the local church in the village of Arnside; the village where she lived and worked for a number of years. It was a nice service and gave me the opportunity to say goodbye to my sister.

After her death, returning from a rat show was always sad. As she liked me to ring and tell her how we got on. She was always thrilled when I said I'd won.

I was so glad my mother had long since passed. If she had known about my brother's sad death and then had to face hearing about the tragic death of her youngest child. It would have killed her. I thank God for my faith, for my strong relationship with Jesus. He kept me sane, and gave me His wonderful peace. A peace the world can't give, or take away

* *
** **

In 2007 I began to write seriously. My chosen genre was fantasy. I had done a certain amount of writing during my singing career, in the times of resting as we all called it … basically out of work. I filled my time between jobs painting and writing.

Now I had the time and opportunity to commit to it. I've always loved fantasy, whether books or films. At the time there was a shortage of Christian fantasy. I hoped along with other authors, I might be able to fill that void.

At first I spent my time trying to find an agent, but with no success. So I decided to go it alone as many authors are doing these days. I've had a fair amount of success. My first book, 'The Shadowed Valley' is written in honour of my sister. It was published in 2012.

I've since written and published eight books. One or two of them are written for young children. I've had the privilege on numerous occasions to go into local schools to read my books to the children … a most enjoyable experience.

I enjoyed my singing career. However, I must say with my painting and now my writing, I feel truly fulfilled. I know this is because God has blessed me in these areas. He is the one who inspires us and sows the seeds of ideas in our hearts and minds. I pray that everything I do will glorify Him, because without Him, I can do nothing.

If success is measured by how much money you make, then I am not a success. But if it is measured by the joy I get out of it, and in knowing there are many who are blessed by my work, whether paintings or books. Then I am truly successful. God is the great creator. We His children do our best to copy what He places within us. It's all about Him, not us.

This is why I no longer worry about worldly success. Yes, at first I admit, I struggled and strove to succeed. I wanted the fame and the money that goes along with it, but as I've grown in physical age and also spiritually. I no longer feel the drive to prostitute my God given talents on the world's stage. I have learned the lesson, to simply enjoy what I have been privileged to do and to be sure that God gets the glory.

I am happy that people enjoy my art and want to read my books. I have given away more books than I have sold and it's a blessing to do it. The knowledge that my books are all over the world, is enough for me.

My only sadness, is that my mother died not knowing what I'd achieved. I hope she would have been proud of me. It was all I'd ever wanted … to make her proud and to know she loved me.

In the last year's we spent together, I know she did. We had grown close and enjoyed a loving mother and daughter relationship. There is a scripture I was given as a young Christian. **God restores the years the locusts have eaten**. Joel 2 v 25. I'm sure she would have enjoyed reading my books.

It's exciting and a real blessing when someone tells you how much they enjoyed a book you have written. If anyone reading this, feels they have a book inside them. Then write it. It could have a positive effect on someone else's life.

In August of 2007 we had some happy news. Keith's son Matthew was going to marry his girlfriend Judelle. She is a lovely young woman and comes from a Christian family. I was so pleased for Keith. It was a lovely wedding, the sun shone for the happy couple.

Keith is proud of Matthew with good cause. He's a fine man, hardworking and extremely clever. He excels at whatever he turns his hand to. We were both thrilled when after a few years they told us they were having a baby. When little Joshua was born, Keith was over the moon, I was delighted for him. He was a grandfather! I don't think he ever imagined such an event happening.

Unfortunately, they live a long way from us, so we don't get to see them as much as we would like.

* *
** **

It's always a blessing to receive good news, especially after coping with so much tragedy.

But little did we know what was to come. So often you hear non-Christians say things like. 'Christianity is nothing more than a crutch for weak people.' Well I am happy to be weak, because it showed me how strong my God is and as it turned out, I was going to need all my heavenly Father's support and help. For my part I had to trust Him completely and hold onto my faith. There was a trial coming that would test every ounce of faith and devotion I possessed.

I understand why in the Bible we read, **Sufficient unto the day is the evil thereof,** Matt 6 v 34. God's word encourages us to live one day at a time. We need to forget the past, and not look too far into the future, but concentrate on the present. It's enough for us to cope with. The future is not for us to worry about. God holds the future.

Yes, there are times when plans have to be made, but they should be made prayerfully in partnership with God. It's for Him to say yes or no. His timing is always perfect. Our part is to listen and heed His voice. That way there is less possibility of making a mistake or taking the wrong path. It's not easy as I know to my cost.

I am still a person who struggles a little with patience. In my enthusiasm I tend to rush ahead. If I am wrong I have to pay the cost. It's much less painful to wait upon God. Listen for His still small voice before rushing into the unknown.

Chapter 14

MANTEL

For the next few years, nothing noteworthy occurred. So I have skipped to the incident that has affected my life in more ways than I can say and not only me, but Keith also. In April 2013 I went to my GP complaining about swellings under my chin. Whenever I was under the weather or had some kind of infection they would increase in size. I didn't know what they were and I didn't like it. They weren't painful, just rather unsightly.

The Doctor made an appointment for me to see someone at the Walsgrave hospital in Coventry.

On 24th April I went to the hospital with my friend Ruth. For some reason Keith couldn't come with me. When my time came to be seen, I went into a darkened room and lay on the bed. The Doctor put some jell stuff on my neck and went over my neck with some sort of hand scanner. While he was doing it he looked at a screen. I asked if he could see the lump. He said yes and told me there was more than one.

He decided he needed to investigate further and was going to do a needle biopsy. He sent me back out to wait with Ruth while he prepared. I was nervous about the procedure. *Would it be painful*? Receiving the aesthetic was a little uncomfortable, but the rest of the procedure was fine. Once it was all over, he told me they would be in touch.

The weeks went by and I heard nothing from the hospital or my GP. Eventually, I decided to ring the hospital and see if they had any results from the test. I was told everything was fine. So content with the news I decided I would have to live with the swellings.

Strangely, in September 2014 I received a letter from the breast screening clinic at the George Eliot our local hospital, inviting me to go for a mammogram. Apparently, my name along with a number of other women of a certain age had been chosen by computer to have the test.

For a number of years I had not bothered to go, but for some reason this time I felt I should. I realise now God was nudging me. As we ladies know, mammograms are not particularly pleasant, but once it was done I left the hospital, happy in the knowledge I would receive the usual letter telling me I was okay.

A few days later a letter arrived from the hospital to say they had found anomalies. This was not what I expected, but I assumed I would have another check and all would be well.

Keith and I arrived at the breast clinic in our local hospital. We were quite relaxed. However, when the nurse saw me, she said, "What are you doing here? You should be at the Walsgrave in Coventry."

I hadn't realized and wrongly assumed the appointment was for another mammogram in my local hospital. She told us not to panic, but to get to the hospital as soon as possible and she would ring them to say we were on our way.

Both Keith and I were a little concerned as we drove to the hospital. Neither of us understood why we had to go to the Walsgrave. I felt it didn't bode well, but I didn't share my thoughts with Keith. I didn't want to worry him. When we arrived at the hospital we hurried to the breast clinic. We were both breathing heavily and feeling a bit stressed.

The receptionist gave me a form to fill in. One of the questions was how anxious are you? It went from one to ten. Oblivious of what was to come, I smiled at Keith and said, "I'll tick number five, that's the number of Grace."

No sooner had I handed the form back to the receptionist than I was called in. Poor Keith had to sit and wait. Two nurses greeted me as I entered the room. It was quite dark. I was asked to remove my top and lie on the bed. The nurse told me they were going to take biopsies from under each of my arms. She spread the jelly stuff on my armpits and then scanned. When that was done, she gave me a local anaesthetic and proceeded with the biopsy. She took three biopsies from under each armpit.

Apart from the anaesthetic injection it was painless. Although, when she had taken biopsies from one armpit and went to put the anaesthetic in the other, the needle broke, squirting anaesthetic everywhere. It just missed going in my eye. She apologised, but there was no harm done. Although, I often wonder what would have happened had it gone in my eye.

Once the small wounds were dressed, Keith and I were taken to a pleasant room and given a much needed cup of tea. When I told him what had been done. The poor man looked as shocked as me.

When we finished our tea the nurse returned and asked me which hospital I preferred to attend. Feeling confused and a little out of it, I said I would prefer our local hospital. At the time I didn't question why she needed to know this. I suppose I assumed it was for the biopsy results. I was concerned, but happily oblivious to the seriousness of my situation.

We both were. The phrase, like lambs to the slaughter comes to mind.

On the way home from the hospital, I rang Ruth and told her what had happened. I was instantly covered by a blanket of prayer. It had been a strange and rather traumatic day. My underarms were a little sore, but that night I slept well. I had no idea what was wrong with me. Why all of a sudden I had to go through these strange and rather scary procedures. Nevertheless, as I waited for the results, I felt as though God had enveloped me in a comforting blanket of peace.

A day later, Keith and I, David and Ruth went to Paula's for a meal. We had a lovely evening. But then, dinner at Paula's is always brilliant. I shared with her what had happened at the Walsgrave, but not knowing the results there was little I could tell her. Like all of us, she was concerned.

I have been blessed with wonderful friends. Most of my biological family are gone. I consider my Christian brothers and sisters my family. David, Ruth and Paula are my go too people, along with other precious friends, like Pauline and her husband Ron and Joy and Bill. I love them all dearly. The body of Christ is awesome and the prayers of the saints powerful and uplifting.

On the 16th of October, I received a letter from our local hospital. I had an appointment for the next day at the breast clinic. The results had come about the biopsy. I would be lying if I said I wasn't anxious, we both were.

I was called to see the Doctor. As I sat down he asked if I was alone. I told him my husband was in the waiting room. The Doctor told the nurse to go and fetch him. If I had any doubts as to the seriousness of my situation, seeing the nurse hurry from the room to fetch Keith confirmed, whatever was wrong was serious … something they didn't want me to hear on my own. Poor Keith, we sat together holding hands and staring anxiously at the Doctor.

The Doctor said, "I am really sorry to have to tell you this, but you have cancer, Non-Hodgkin's Lymphoma."

He asked me if I'd heard of it. I wasn't sure if I had and being in a state of shock, I nodded. I sat there and listened to him talking about chemo and a bone marrow biopsy. I guess he saw the panic on my face, because he quickly reassured me and told me I didn't need to worry. Everything that had to be done would be arranged for me. I was given a blood form and told to go to the path lab.

As I waited for the blood test my mind whirled with confused thoughts and I admit a little fear. I had just been told I had cancer. Keith and I sat together in silence. We neither of us knew what to say. While we waited, I sent my friend Ruth a text. I could tell by her reply she was as shocked as us. When we eventually got home they came round to see us and prayed. They are such a blessing to us.

For the next few days, I felt amazingly calm

and continued to do those things I had planned. Coffee with friends or lunch, whatever had been planned before receiving the awful news. It was weird, I was supposedly ill, yet I felt fine and so peaceful.

*** ***

A few days later I felt as though I was on a crazy … scary merry- go- round. My feet didn't touch the ground. It was one appointment after another. I was sent for another blood test and then on the 23rd of October I had an appointment with the oncologist. The appointment was in the morning, at eleven fifteen, but we were warned it could be a long wait as she had fitted me in as an emergency. We didn't get to see her until around four pm.

However, the clinic was comfortable, light and airy. So different from the horrid place my poor mother had to go to. The only negative, was the fact that the actual treatment ward was visible from the waiting area. You could see the many patients receiving their chemo and hear the constant beeping from the machines. I found it all a bit unnerving and struggled to believe I had become part of it.

Nevertheless, I felt surprisingly calm, if a little restless. I found it hard to sit still. I just wanted to see the Doctor and find out what was wrong with me. When at last my name was called, I was pretty hyper, trembling with supressed anxiety and yet inside strangely calm ... weird.

I breezed into her office, proclaiming, "I don't know why I'm here. I feel fine. There's nothing wrong with me."

Smiling, she ushered us in. "I'm afraid there is, "she said. I could hear the sympathy in her voice. She was friendly and open. I liked her instantly. For a brief while we talked. I did my best to answer her questions. She wanted to know about my family and about Keith and myself.

After a while she looked at her computer screen and proceeded to explain exactly what my situation was. She told me I had stage four, Mantel Cell Lymphoma, which is a rare form of Non-Hodgkin's Lymphoma. Mostly, it afflicts older men, but occasionally as in my case, women.

She told us, it is aggressive and incurable. It can be halted, but it will return and each time it does, it is worse. I didn't know what to say, I just looked at Keith. I felt strangely calm. I knew I must lean fully upon God and trust Him completely.

The oncologist said she would book me in for a scan and that I needed to have a bone marrow biopsy. The thought of the biopsy terrified me. She wanted me to have it within the next few days. But I pleaded to have it after Christmas, she agreed.

I was so grateful for the prayers of my Christian family. I felt as though this wasn't happening … wasn't real. I had such a deep sense of peace.

On the Saturday after seeing the oncologist, we had an early phone call from the hospital. I was booked in for a scan. Unfortunately, I'd had a small breakfast, but they said it would be alright, as the scan was booked for four pm.

In the evening we were to go to David's church. They were celebrating the many years he had ministered there. I was tired, but I wanted to go, it was a special night for David. I was to sing with Ruth, which I was looking forward to.

When we arrived I felt they were relieved to see us. I enjoyed singing with Ruth. We had chosen a Hymn I absolutely love. '**The Love of God is greater far, than tongue or pen can ever tell**.' A beautiful hymn and the words were so appropriate to how I felt.

It was a lovely evening, celebrating and praising our awesome God. I was so glad I managed to go. For a while I was able to forget the scan and everything else and just be with my friends, my brothers and sisters in Christ. I think it helped Keith as well.

Those of us, who are suffering, get so caught up in our own trouble. We tend to forget our loved ones, our family. It was hard and scary for me. How much harder was it for Keith? All he could do was standby and support as best could, which he certainly did.

I know he would have given anything to be able to help in a practical way. He would often say, "I wish I could go through this for you." It was a sweet sentiment, but no way would I want him to go through it. However, he could pray and that he did.

Chapter 15

On November the twelfth, I saw the oncologist. She had the results from my scan. There was good and bad news. I had lymph nodes in my lungs, stomach and spleen, as well as my neck. It was strange to hear that and yet to feel perfectly well. She said as I was in good health, they would hold off on treatment and put me on watch and wait, for as long as possible

I have since learned, with MCL the longer you can leave it the better. It is best not to wake the sleeping beast (as we mantel sufferers call it) until it's really necessary. Once you start the treatment the battle is on.

I thanked God that I was healthy enough to go on watch and wait. I prayed, as did my husband and my friends, that God willing I would remain on it for a good long time.

Having the option of watch and wait is brilliant, the only negative I felt, was knowing it was temporary. It felt like a sword was hanging over my head. Sometimes, I struggled with the knowledge that inside me there was a horrible sickness waiting to show its evil hand.

It was worse at night. During the day I could keep busying writing my books and socialising with friends. But at night, my powerful imagination filled my mind with all sorts of frightening scenarios. It was hard and there were some nights I wept. I would pray and seek God's comfort and strength, He never let me down.

Prayer was my weapon. It was all I had to fight this battle. And what a powerful weapon it is. When I couldn't pray for myself, others prayed for me. The battle is not ours its Gods. When I was at my weakest, He was my strength. I could never fight this awful disease without His strength, peace and love.

How others do it without Him, I don't know. Maybe, people will think I'm weak, that my belief in God is a crutch. I don't care what they think. The weaker I am, the more deeply I know Him and the power of His might and comforting presence.

God is the father I never had, the beautiful,

tangible person who promised to never leave me or forsake me. In place of the word forsake, I choose the word, reject. Unlike my earthly fathers, He never has. And I know, He never will.

* *
** **

The remainder of 2014 flew by, Christmas came and went. Seeing in the New Year 2015 brought with it a little anxiety. I was to experience my first bone marrow biopsy. It was booked for the morning of the 9th of January. I admit I was scared.

As it turned out, yes, it was unpleasant, but not as bad as I anticipated. I was given a local anaesthetic. I find sometimes they can be more painful than the actual procedure, although in this case once the Doctor began extracting the bone marrow, it was most uncomfortable. I can't tell you what it felt like, but I couldn't help groaning. It felt as though my life was being pulled out of me. Not that I have any idea how that would feel.

Once it was over the area was dressed and I had a cup of tea. I've had a few more since then, so I'm no longer quite so nervous about it. Nevertheless, it's still one of the procedures I dread the most and waiting for the results was nerve-racking.

However, when I saw my oncologist the

results were good. So I could remain on watch and wait for another three months. Keith and I were delighted and gave God all the praise.

In those three months I kept busy with writing and publishing. I also had the privilege of going into a local school to read one of my books to a class of seven year olds. I was going to read the whole book, so I went to the school once a week. I love being able to do this. Children are so receptive. I enjoyed it and the children did too.

It's amazing how quickly the months fly by. It was September and I was booked to see my oncologist, but she was away. I didn't know and it upset me. I was booked to see one of the Doctors, who had taken care of my mother, but I didn't want to. The receptionist tried to get me to make another appointment. But if I couldn't see my oncologist on that day, I didn't want to see anyone else, so I left in a bit of a paddy. They called after me, but I ignored them.

Poor Keith, he didn't know what to do, so he followed me to the car. All the while I was ranting on about not caring if I get treatment or not.

My anger was sparked I believe, by the fact that the doctor I was booked to see had been one of two who had looked after my mother.

It's distressing, as each time you have an appointment to see the oncologist; you are on tender-hooks, as you never know what the outcome will be. Fellow cancer sufferers will know what I mean. You steel yourself for the worst news. I liked and trusted my oncologist. I didn't want to see anyone else, especially the Doctors who had taken care of my mother.

I was distressed and when I got home I burst into tears as I tried to explain to Keith how I felt. He understood, as he had been with mother and me many times when she went for her appointments. He remembered the two Doctors and the horrid, dark depressing clinic.

I had nothing against mother's Doctors. They looked after her well. I just didn't want to follow in my mother's footsteps. I needed to walk my own path. It was bad enough trying to cope with my own situation, without being constantly reminded of my mother's suffering.

My battle with cancer is personal, as it is for all who suffer from this dreadful disease. My relationship with my God is deeply personal. On a simple level, He loves me and I love Him with all my heart. I am grateful for His protection, and love. All through my treatment I was aware of Him watching over me. He kept me safe and gave me the strength I needed to stay strong in my faith and to trust Him.

I firmly believe that God has put me in the care of my oncologist. He helped me to find favour with her. I trust her. Each time I saw her I felt reassured. No way was I going to see anyone else.

On that first day of meeting her, I mentioned palliative care. She was not pleased. "There will be no talk of palliative care," she said. "When the time comes, I have a plan."

A week or so later I received a letter from the hospital. It was a new appointment to see her. I must admit, I felt a little ashamed of my behaviour the last time I was there. As soon as we arrived at the clinic, I checked who I was to see. Hearing it was my oncologist, I breathed a sigh of relief.

When we went in to see her, I quickly apologised for my behaviour. She smiled and told me not to worry. She understood and advised me to make sure I always saw her. She said she would also write it on the folder containing my notes.

There was more encouraging news. She told us my bloods were good. So I could remain on watch and wait. This time we were happy as we drove home.

I had to smile though. I found out that after walking out of the hospital in a huff, I had acquired the reputation of being an escapee. Well, I always have been a bit of a rebel.

Chapter 16

On the 15th of February I had another appointment with my oncologist. The news was not quite so good, but she gave me another two months on watch and wait. It looked like I was close to starting treatment. I had no idea what was going to happen, but I must admit I dreaded it.

As it turned out I couldn't enjoy the two months she gave me. I had a pain under my left shoulder blade and began to feel extremely tired and unwell. On Sunday the 28th the church prayed for me and Keith. A young Korean woman in the congregation had a picture for me. She said I was swimming in water that was too deep, but I was being held up by God. That blessed me.

On Tuesday, I rang my Oncologist and told her how I felt. She was not surprised and told me to come to the clinic the next day. Boy, it was a long day and there was so much to take in! Half of what she told me, I didn't understand.

She said even though I was 69, I was strong within myself and had a positive attitude. She felt I would cope with an extremely aggressive treatment, mostly reserved for younger patients. This had been the plan she had talked about when I first met her.

She didn't know that my positive attitude was down to my faith in God and the fact that I was covered with prayer. When she reeled off everything she had planned for me, I thought about the Korean woman's picture. It was certainly appropriate to my situation. Hearing the treatment I was to have, I felt as though I was drowning. Nevertheless, I trusted God and the prayers of my Christian family. I was scared and yet at the same time I felt the peace of God so strongly.

When one of the nurses took me aside to explain things further, I confess I became emotional. It wasn't easy for Keith either. For months we had sat in the waiting room waiting to see the oncologist and as I said before there was no door to the treatment room, so you could see what was going on. At those times it didn't occur to me that one day I would be joining all those patients. I think the urge to survive makes us block out things that are unpleasant.

So on the 3rd of March I started treatment. It was Nordic Protocal, Maxi chop and high dose Cytarabine and I had Rituximab. Later on I was going to have a stem cell transplant. Everything was being done, that could be done to help me.

On the scary morning I started chemo. Keith and a friend sat with me. It wasn't as bad as I expected. Actually, I'm not sure what I expected. I had told the nurses I tend to be a sickie person, so I was given something to help with that and anti-sickness meds to take home.

There was one funny moment during that first treatment. I needed the toilet, so I went to the one across from where I was sitting. When I returned to my chair, Keith and my friend were laughing. Keith told me my Oncologist had come into the ward. Seeing the empty chair, she asked where I was. Keith told her and apparently she said. "Oh no, there's a door in there, she may try to escape." We all laughed and laughter is good medicine.

When we got home, I felt okay but that soon changed I spent the whole night vomiting. Don't ask me why I didn't take the anti-sickness meds, I don't know, probably, because I'd felt okay. I've never been a person who likes taking medication, not if I can help it. Once the sickness started, it wouldn't stop. Poor Keith, it was a dreadful night for both of us.

In the morning we rang the unit, they told us to come straight in. Once I had two bags of saline, I felt better. My oncologist popped in to see me. She and the nurses told me to make sure I always took the sickness meds after I had chemo. Believe me, after that experience I did. The next day I felt better as both Keith and I slept well.

A few days after this, we returned to the unit to be shown how to give myself injections in the stomach. I couldn't do it. Keith bless him was the brave one, he did it for me. I have to say, he did it better than some of the nurses.

As this nightmare progressed, I realized how blessed I was to have Keith. He was there for me without question. During the coming months of ongoing treatment, I heard stories from other patients I met. They told me that their partners or boyfriends left them, the minute they found out they had cancer. It's so sad and made me realise how blessed I was to have my dear husband, my awesome heavenly father and my wonderful church family.

After the first treatment I felt okay, but tired. During these few days in-between treatment I made an empowering decision. I called my hairdresser and asked her to come and shave my head. It really didn't bother me. I wasn't blessed with a thick head of hair anyway.

The funny thing was, I was taking a shower and to my surprise and in a way, amusement. The hair down below fell out as I washed. I yelled for

Keith, we were both surprised. It was not something we expected. I had thought I would only lose the hair on my head. Not long after that I lost my eyebrows and eyelashes. One of the good things to come out of all this hair loss, was I no longer had to shave my legs, which was great ... smooth legs. It's good to be able to find positives in every situation.

Something else I enjoyed was choosing my chemo hats. There is a good choice and some of them are lovely. I enjoyed wearing them. It was also fun choosing a wig. We got it cheaper due to the cancer. With Keith's help, I chose a pale blond wig in the style of a bob. My hairdresser came and trimmed it for me. She also gave me a hairdressing head to put on. I felt really good wearing it. So there were good things to be thankful for.

In-between my first and next treatment, I did my best to get out and about and see my friends. I also went back to church. It was the first time in a while. I felt a bit awkward and nervous, but everyone was so kind. I soon felt at home. It was good to tell them how much I appreciated their prayers.

On the 22 March I saw my oncologist. She was pleased with how well I was coping. She told me on the coming Thursday I would be going to the Walsgrave hospital. It would seem I was going to alternate between our local hospital and the Walsgrave, where I would be having a different chemo.

On the Thursday the Walsgrave rang and told

me I was expected. Can't say I was looking forward to it. Unlike our hospital, the Walsgrave is huge with a large cancer ward for both men and women.

When I arrived and saw the consultant, he told me what to expect. I was to be given eye drops every two hours while undergoing the chemo to protect my eyes. I was able to do it myself as the nurses were busy. If I did it, I knew it would be done at the right time. I certainly didn't want my eyes damaged.

I was in the hospital from Thursday night until I went home on the Saturday. I left with a load of medication and what was left of the eye drops. For the first time I began to feel unwell. I was weak and struggling to eat or drink. Everything I tried tasted foul. One of the other patients suggested I try pineapple juice. We bought a carton and I couldn't wait to try it. Sadly, it was gross, it tasted like cheese. The only liquid I could stomach was sparkling water. Food became more of a challenge.

On the Wednesday after leaving the hospital I went with Keith to Asda. I was grateful for the trolley. I used it as a support. While we were going round my oncologist rang my mobile. I knew I shouldn't have been out, but I needed a change of scene. She said she suddenly thought about me and needed to check that the Walsgrave had sent me home with the tummy injections … they hadn't.

She told me to send Keith to her unit and she would leave out a prescription for him. I said I would go with him. She said, "No, you have no immunity." She assumed I was at home, I prayed no voice would come over the loud speakers in Asda and say something like, "Don't forget, you can get two for one in the biscuit aisle," while she was on the phone.

I had no idea how vulnerable I was. I had no immunity and was extremely weak. Nevertheless, we couldn't help laughing as we hurried back to the car. I felt like a naughty child playing hooky from school.

Keith dropped me home and left me to put the shopping away while he drove to the hospital to get the injections. Alone in the house, I realised only one person could have nudged the oncologist to phone me. I was thrilled at the way God looked after me and how caring my oncologist was. Between the two of them, but especially God, I felt cared for and safe. My father was watching out for me. And believe me there would be other times when I was more than grateful for His care and attention.

A few days later on the 4th of April, having previously had a blood test, things were not so good and I had to go to the hospital. A friend picked me up and got me there for nine thirty. My oncologist had ordered a blood transfusion. It was the first one I'd had. I was intrigued that both the blood and the platelets had to be irradiated.

The transfusion was followed by a blood test and then I saw the oncologist. She was not happy and they decided to keep me in. Probably, just as well as the next day I was unwell with a high temperature. I was given antibiotics, along with another blood and platelet transfusion. It turns out I was allergic to the irradiated platelets. Each time I had it, I would get sever hives. But not so much this time as I was already having antibiotics.

It was nice to be in our local hospital and everyone was so nice, even so, I couldn't wait to get home. On the third day, I became upset. The first cannula I had in the back of my hand had to be changed and no one in the ward seemed able to do it. The constant trying made the back of my hand sore and bruised, it stressed me out.

I'd had enough and when the doctors came to see me, I insisted I wanted to go home. Fortunately, I was much improved and they decided to send me home with oral antibiotics. I could hardly wait for Keith to come and pick me up.

On the 14th of April I was back in the local hospital for more chemo. Keith dropped me and my friend Paula came and sat with me. It was a long day. I was grateful for her company. Good friends are to be loved and valued. I have good friends and I love them and thank God for them.

Chapter 17

On the 5th of May, I was due to have another scary procedure. I was to have a Hickman line fitted. Keith and I turned up at the Walsgrave as instructed for eight am. Due to nerves I hadn't slept well. Nevertheless, I steeled myself to be brave and I could feel God's presence with me, so I was reasonably calm when they wheeled me down to the theatre.

My bed was parked with a couple of others outside the theatre. It seemed a long wait. I could feel myself getting anxious. The Doctor doing the procedure came to me and apologised. He explained he couldn't do it as my platelets were too low. I was annoyed and frustrated.

I was taken back to the ward where Keith was patiently waiting, along with my oncologist and the head nurse in charge of this particular procedure. This nurse was the lady who organises the stem cell treatments, which is why I needed the Hickman line. Both she and my oncologist were annoyed. They both felt the surgeon was being overly cautious.

The head nurse asked me if I wanted to go home, or stay in and have the chemo I was due to have in about a week's time. I looked from one to the other. I knew my oncologist didn't mind what I chose to do, but I felt the nurse wanted me to stay and have the chemo. However, I wanted to go home, so they let me.

I was annoyed, that due to my platelets I couldn't have the line in. I was all prepared and ready to have it done. Now I would have to wait until the bloods were improved. But God knows what is best and I was learning to trust Him.

For the next few days things got a little hectic. Half the time I didn't know which hospital I was supposed to attend. On the 11th May, my friend Ruth went with me to the Walsgrave. I had a blood test and then saw a Doctor who explained what would happen prior to and then during the stem cell transplant. I have to say it sounded frightening. They said it can be dangerous and I had to sign a form to say I agreed to have it.

I had a lot to think about as we drove back to

Nuneaton. Ruth dropped me at the Mary Anne Evens Hospice situated in the grounds of our local hospital. I had been invited to go there for the day every Wednesday. It was a lovely place and so peaceful. The staff were wonderful and it was nice to be among people who themselves were poorly and understood what we were all going through.

The day would be spent doing crafts or painting, or if you preferred just resting in the comfy armchairs and talking. There was tea, coffee and biscuits and at lunch time a delicious home cooked meal. We were each allowed to go there for sixteen weeks. I guess there was a long que of people waiting to attend. I was fortunate to be able to go twice.

While I was there I learned how to make some pretty jewellery and renewed my love of painting. I enjoyed the experience and got to know the staff, they are lovely people. Unfortunately, it's a day hospice. They had wanted to have beds and do palliative care, but sadly it was too costly.

On this particular day I was grateful to be there. I immersed myself in the crafts and tried to forget the unpleasant information I had received about having the stem cells. Later when Keith picked me up to go home I told him what the hospital had said. The poor man was as disturbed as I was about it.

However, we both agreed, this procedure was some way ahead and it was enough for us to cope with what was going on now. I had a Hickman line to be fitted and more chemo to cope with. As the Bible says, **Sufficient unto the day is the evil there of.** Matt 6 v 34.

I took a few deep breaths as on the way home, Keith told me that while I was at the Hospice the head nurse had rung from the Walsgrave to say I was expected the next morning at eight am to have the line put in and after that I would be staying for the usual chemo treatment. Knowing what tomorrow held, I had a restless night.

We were up early and got underway. We hoped to avoid traffic on the motorway and also be able to park once we arrived at the hospital, most of the time it was an absolute nightmare trying to find a space. The hospital is huge, but as is usual, the parking is never enough for the amount of people booked in for appointments. However, arriving that early in the morning we had no trouble.

Once again I was wheeled down to the theatre and this time there were no problems with my blood. A nurse put a mask over my face, so that I could breathe the gas. Not something I enjoyed as I'm claustrophobic.

I was given a local anaesthetic in my breast and then a thick tube was inserted under my skin and pushed into the large vein that drains into the heart. I can't say it was painful, but I could feel it pushing through the flesh, which felt unpleasantly weird. Let's put it this way, I didn't enjoy it. It's not something I would rush to have done again. But it was necessary, due to the fact I would be having stem cells.

I was relieved when it was all over and they wheeled me back to the cancer unit. I was pleased to see Keith and in need of a cup of tea and a biscuit. I was supposed to stay in and continue treatment, but an emergency patient took my bed, so we went home, which I was pleased about. We were told to ring the next morning. Fortunately, I didn't have to return until the next day Saturday. I had the chemo and was allowed to go home on the Sunday.

It felt weird having two thick plastic tubes hanging out of my breast. Each one had what is called a small lumen on the end which are turned on and off as blood is needed for testing or for chemo and other transfusions to be put through it. This is the best way I can describe it.

A couple of days after having the line inserted, I had to go to my local cancer unit so that the nurse could check and clean the lumen. I was more fortunate than some in that my blood flowed freely, which was important when the time came to harvest my stem cells. It was because of this that the plastic tubing was on the thick side.

The next day I spent relaxing, I felt pretty drained. Eating and drinking were a real problem and my weight was dropping off. Our friend Sue, who before treatment used to come for a meal on Wednesday evenings, rang me to say she'd had a picture for me from the Lord. In the picture she saw me covered with a silver cloth. She felt it was conveying God's protection over me. I was more than happy to receive it. I thanked the Lord for always being with me and giving me His wonderful peace.

For the next few days I had to go to the local hospital for injections and blood and platelet transfusions. I believe the injections were to help the increase of my stem cells. On the Thursday evening, after the blood transfusion I felt unwell and had a high temperature.

Keith took me to the hospital, they kept me in. I was shattered by the time I got up to the ward. All I wanted to do was sleep. I was given a room to myself, which was nice. When the porter wheeled me in a nurse was waiting for me. She told me she was an agency nurse. She was kind and helpful.

The bag of fluid attached to my arm was empty, so she took it away and separated the tube from the cannula which was in the inside of my left arm, in the vein that's used for blood tests. Without the plastic tube attached to the cannula, I could sleep more comfortably.

I had to have the cannula in my arm, because no one else is allowed to touch the Hickman line, apart from the nurses in the cancer unit.

She gave me a hospital gown and wished me goodnight. Exhausted, I snuggled down and instantly fell into a deep sleep. Later for some reason I woke up, I looked at the clock it was four am. I couldn't understand why I felt cold and strangely wet. Pushing the sheet back I looked at my hand, it was wet and pink. I threw off the sheet and nearly screamed.

Thinking I'd had some sort of nightmare I switched on the light. With no exaggeration, what I saw was like something out a horror movie. I was covered in blood. Everything was soaked red, the bedding, my hospital gown, my underwear, and even the pillow.

My heart raced with fear, it pounded in my head. Desperate, I quickly looked at the Hickman line. Had I accidently pulled it out in my sleep? Terrified of what I might have done I pressed the emergency bell, I kept pressing it! I was way beyond panic now. Blood was still coming from somewhere, but I was too frightened and half asleep to figure it out.

To my relief, the door opened and the nurse who had greeted me when I arrived rushed in. Seeing the mess and the state I was in she looked horrified. Right away she knew what the problem was. Grabbing my arm she secured the cannula and stopped the blood flow. The bed was stripped and remade. What I was wearing was removed and she helped to clean me up and find me another gown. The bedding, everything was thrown into the laundry. My underwear I threw in the bin.

I can't imagine what the laundry people thought when they received the blood soaked bedding. I would love to have been a fly on the wall. I guess it's possible it was all thrown away. From the state of it, it looked as though someone had been violently murdered and had bled to death.

Mind you, that could so easily have happened, if I had not woken up. No, I'm not exaggerating. It was terrifying and an experience that remains with me.

As I lay in the clean bed, shivering with the cold and loss of blood, I realised I had God to thank that I was okay and safe in bed. I know He woke me and helped me to remain reasonably calm.

I didn't see the agency nurse again and no one said anything about it, neither did I. I guess I could have made a fuss, but what would have been the point. Accidents happen and no real harm was done. I have only ever received kind and caring treatment from everyone at the hospital. So I said nothing, accept to tell the Doctors when they came to see me. From the way they responded it was obvious they already knew.

After another blood transfusion and a warm shower, I felt better and spent a pleasant and restful time recovering from the trauma of the night before. When I rang Keith and told him what had happened, he was naturally shocked and concerned. He came to the hospital and spent some time with me. When he left to go home, all I wanted to do was go with him. Unfortunately, I had to wait until the next day as the Doctors needed to be sure I was okay. Thank the Lord the next day I was discharged and Keith came and took me home.

The next few days passed uneventfully. I managed to find a man to do the garden for us. Neither of us had the time or the energy to keep on top of it. The man was nice and did a good job.

One morning I woke with extremely pink cheeks and the next day I developed an irritating dry cough. I called it chemo cough as apparently that's what caused it. I prayed it wouldn't last long as it was most annoying, especially at night.

I began another course of tummy injections I assumed to stimulate my stem cells. I was beginning to feel like a pin cushion. I had a huge bruise on my stomach thanks to one of the nurses. Keith did a better job.

On Saturday the eleventh of June, I felt really poorly. I had no appetite and a high temperature. I lay on the couch covered with a blanket. Poor Keith was worried. We rang my oncologist and she told him to take me to the Walsgrave and she would contact them in advance.

With all I had been through, I had never felt this ill. Unfortunately, it was close to the time for my stem cell harvesting. The next day I felt a little better, but emotional. The head stem cell nurse came to see me. She said my blood count was low which depressed me as it affected the stem cell count. David and Ruth came to see me, which cheered me up. We always have a laugh when we get together.

The next day the stem cell nurse came again. She took some blood. Unfortunately the news wasn't good. There was only one cell. However, her positive attitude gave me confidence. When she left a Doctor came, he said I was low in potassium and I was still at risk of a fever. I told him I would eat bananas. He smiled, but ordered a transfusion, which is much better than having to take Potassium tablets in water, as it tastes foul.

The time for my stem cell harvesting was getting close. I was fortunate to be able to use my own stem cells. Although going by the blood tests, things weren't looking too good. Nevertheless, I determined to remain positive. I knew the nurse would do everything she could to help me. But more importantly, I knew God was on my side. I trusted Him to help. He knew my desperate need and by faith I believed He would help me.

Chapter 18

For the stem cell harvesting, I had to go to Warwick. It's a small hospital, but the cancer unit there is where the stem cells are harvested. Neither Keith nor I knew where the hospital was or how to get there. There was no ambulance to take me, so I had to make my own way. Added to the transport problem, Keith was unwell. So I was concerned about dragging him all the way to the Walsgrave and then struggling to find our way to the Warwick hospital.

But as always God supplied my need, our lovely friend Sue offered to take me. She works in

Warwick and knows the hospital. She arrived early, so before leaving the Walsgrave we went and had a Costa coffee. The café is on the ground floor of the hospital. It was good to relax with her for a brief time before setting off to the other hospital. Unsure if the procedure I was to have would be uncomfortable or a failure, I was naturally anxious.

Sue knew where the hospital was and we found the cancer unit without any problem. It was a separate building from the actual hospital. As she dropped me off we arranged I would phone her when the procedure was over. I found the small stem cell unit and was greeted by extremely friendly people. There were only two, the man who worked the machine and a nurse. The man was nice and it was obvious to me he was proud of what he considered was his machine.

I'm not sure what I was expecting, but I was in a small but pleasant room. The harvesting machine was positioned close to the bed. It was no bigger than a washing machine. Once I was settled on the bed, the nurse cleaned the lumen on the end of my Hickman line and I was attached to the machine.

It was as though my body could hardly wait. Blood began to flow from both my lines before they were properly attached to the machine. The man and the nurse were pleased and seemed relieved. When they told me the sort of trouble some people experience I understood why.

With some poor patients it just didn't work.

Either the blood wouldn't flow or the harvesting was unsuccessful. I felt so sad for them. It meant they had to have donor stem cells, which comes with its own risks. They told me most donor stem cells come from Germany.

Silently, I thanked God my line was working so well and I prayed we would be successful with the harvesting. They needed to collect at the least two thousand cells, preferably more.

I had a lovely day. As I said these two people were so nice, we chatted and laughed. My lunch arrived in a posh paper carrier bag. It consisted of a sandwich of my choice with a bag of crisps and an apple.

The machine fascinated me. The man was happy to explain how it worked. There were three bags, one for blood, one for plasma and one for the stem cells. When the plasma and stem cells were removed from the blood, the blood was transfused back into me. I was intrigued as to how the machine knew which was which ... amazing.

On his laptop he showed me what my stem cells looked like. They were small and round. He explained that once they arrived in Birmingham, they would be dyed purple, for easy identification. Then they would be frozen and stored. I found the whole thing fascinating. I could understand why the man enjoyed what he did. Apart from the fact, that God willing he was saving lives.

I was excited to tell Sue all about it when she

picked me up. She too found it interesting. She dropped me back at the Walsgrave, and said she would be back the next day, as I had to return for more harvesting.

When I arrived back on the ward, there were hardly any nurses about. I had made friends with some of the other patients and they told me it had been a stressful day, with a distinct shortage of staff. Everyone seemed agitated and harassed. Some hadn't received their medication or chemo.

They had already had their evening meal, so I asked one of the nurses if I could have something to eat, she brushed me off. I was tired, the man who harvested my cells warned me the procedure was quite draining and to expect to feel weary. I did and added to that I felt annoyed and neglected.

Without saying anything, I left the ward and went downstairs to the hospital restaurant and bought myself a curry. I shouldn't have had to do it, but it was obvious I was not going get anything to eat if I stayed on the ward.

I felt drained, vulnerable and tearful. I felt even worse when I returned to the ward and the head nurse came to see me. She looked concerned. It seems we only managed to harvest about a thousand cells … not nearly enough. She wanted at least two thousand or more.

Everyone on the ward seemed stressed and unhappy. I pulled my curtains round for some privacy. Sitting on my bed I cried. The night staff had come on and one of the nurses came to me. I tried to explain how I felt. She was sympathetic and understood. She explained that staffing was a problem, but I was not to worry … none of us were to worry. We were not in any danger.

Later that evening the stem cell nurse came with an injection. Apparently, it was powerful and God willing would stimulate my body to produce a larger quantity of cells. That night in bed, I prayed it would work.

The transplant itself was dangerous enough, even more so if I had to have donor cells. This whole situation was raising my stress level, so I guess it was natural to be a little upset. Walking into a serious staffing problem didn't help. But God gave me peace and I slept.

Early the next morning, pretty much before everyone else was awake, I packed my bag. I had decided after the harvesting, I was going home. When the nurse arrived, she kindly made me some toast. After I'd eaten, I hurried downstairs. Sue was waiting for me in the car. When she saw I was carrying my bag she looked a little surprised. I told her after the harvesting I wanted to go home. "Does the hospital know?" She asked. I told her not to worry. As far as I could see, with the situation as it was, one less patient would surely be a help.

She dropped me at the Warwick cancer unit and I made my way to the harvesting room. Again I had an enjoyable day. When the harvesting was done the man told me this time we managed to get over two thousand cells. I was thrilled and we were all relieved. When the harvesting was complete the cells were frozen and taken to somewhere in Birmingham, where they would remain until my transplant.

While I was there the nurse rang, she was delighted with the number we had harvested, but she had noticed in the ward that my belongings were missing. She told the man to make sure I returned to the hospital. I just grinned. I was having one of my escapee moments.

When Sue picked me up she tried to convince me to return to the hospital. I told her I didn't like it there and I wanted to go home. "There's nothing more to be done," I said to reassure her. The poor girl didn't look convinced. But we laughed when she said she wasn't sure who she was more afraid of, the nurse or me.

When we arrived at my house, Keith opened the door. He was talking on the phone. It was the head nurse insisting I return to the hospital, as I still had to have antibiotics. I was annoyed, but there was no point arguing. Having said goodbye to Sue, I went upstairs to freshen up and change. Keith was taking me back to the hospital. It was nice to spend some time with him.

That night I had the antibiotics. Nothing was said about my escape attempt. In the morning a Doctor came and told me I could go home. To say I was relieved was an understatement.

A couple of days after leaving the hospital I saw my oncologist and had my Hickman line cleaned. All was well and for the next few days I rested and enjoyed visits from my friends.

However, on the 1st of June I was back in the Walsgrave for more chemo. I was there for an uneventful few days. I was pleased when Keith took me home. Unfortunately, on the 11th July while at home, I became unwell with a high temperature.

Keith took me to our local hospital and they kept me in. For the first night I had to sleep in a cubical in A and E. I didn't mind as the bed was comfy and I felt so poorly, I was pretty much out of it. In the morning the nurse told me I slept so soundly, I didn't even know when she took my temperature.

Eventually, I was moved to a ward and then into a room by myself. After being in the hospital for three days, the Doctor convinced me to stay for one more night. I was feeling so much better but I agreed. Keith and a friend came to see me, which was nice. It does get boring in the hospital. When I was allowed to go home, life alternated between chemo treatments and line cleaning.

The last time I was at the Walsgrave hospital in between having my stem cells harvested, one of the Doctors had come to see me. He explained a little about the transplant. I asked him how dangerous it really was and did I need to put my house in order?

He replied, "That's something you should have done the moment you were diagnosed. The cancer you have is not curable."

I told him I knew that.

He said the transplant had risks, a possible 1.3% chance of dying. I told him I wasn't afraid of dying. When he left he gave my shoulder a comforting squeeze. I knew the coming transplant could be life threatening, but I tried not to dwell on it. I trusted in God and the prayers of my church family. Whenever I prayed and read my Bible, I would become emotional as God's word touched my spirit. I was strengthened by His presence and the prayers of His people.

Of course there were times when I felt anxious and vulnerable. Especially, as the transplant day approached. But it was at night when the reality of my situation would strike home. We all know things look worse in the dark and quiet of night. At this time we are at the mercy of our thoughts.

Trying to sleep and silence the scary thoughts charging around inside my head was hard. But in the light of dawn I always found knew strength and would thank God for bringing me to a new day, knowing that whatever that day held, He would be with me and help me to face it.

After another round of chemo at the Walsgrave, I was glad to go home. However, it wasn't going to be a restful time as my oncologist had booked a busy week for me. Before having the transplant my Doctors needed to know I was strong enough to cope with it. So I found myself booked in for a rigorous heart check, the results of which were fine, thank the Lord.

I also had to undergo a check on my lungs, which I didn't enjoy. I was put in a small glass cubical with a clip on my nose and told to breathe into a tube as hard as I could. As well as tests to see how long I could hold my breath. I think I mentioned before, that I am seriously claustrophobic … I hated it.

I felt the nurse doing the tests was getting impatient with me, but I was doing my best. I just didn't seem to have the power to breathe as hard as she wanted, or hold my breath long enough. I apologised and politely suggested she take a look at my latest blood tests on her computer. When she returned she nodded at me. She told me my oxygen levels were low and said I could go home. I was more than happy to comply.

I also had to have my kidneys checked. For that I had to return to the Walsgrave, but at least it was only for the day. After giving a urine sample, I was given some kind of special injection. I was pleased to hear my kidneys were fine. It was a long day, by the time Keith and I got home we were both tired.

On the 9th of August I was supposed to go to the Walsgrave and have the last chemo treatment before having the transplant. But the nurse rang to say unfortunately no bed was available. She reassured me all was well and it was quite safe for me to wait a few more days.

Nevertheless, I felt agitated. It reminded me of the day I was meant to have the Hickman line, but that was postponed due to my platelet count.

I had built myself up in preparation and now I had to try and remain calm and wait. It was frustrating. The word patience comes to mind! But understandably, all I wanted was to get it done and over with, whatever the outcome might be. My favourite scripture all through the eighteen months of treatment was, **for to me to live is Christ and to die is gain.** Philippians 1 v 21.

It's a scripture that truly expresses how I feel. I'm not afraid to die. But I admit, as a human being, knowing how nasty this particular cancer is, I do have concerns as to the way I might die. Nevertheless, I can honestly say, as a child of God. Whatever happens, I am in a win, win situation. As Philippians 1 v21 makes abundantly clear

Chapter 19

On the 16th of August having had to wait a week, I was called into the hospital. After so many months of chemo, it was time to have the stem cell transplant. Was I anxious? Oh yes. During my numerous times in the hospital, I got to know and like, two particular nurses. This time, whenever they were on duty, they gave me sympathetic looks and occasional words of encouragement. One particular nurse, a sweet young lady held my hand and advised me that when the time came, I should try to eat as many ice cubes as I could. I had no idea what she was talking about. I soon found out.

For the first week, I remained on the ward with the other patients, having my normal chemo treatment, if you can call it that. This kind off lulled me into a false sense of security.

I had two particular friends in the ward. We were often in there at the same time. Both of whom were having stem cells after me. The younger woman was having the cells her daughter donated. My older friend Val was being given stem cells from a donor in Germany. This was common, if you couldn't have your own or from a close relative, then you were given cells from Germany.

With both of these options rejection medication had to be taken. Those like me who were fortunate to have their own cells didn't have this added problem. Nevertheless, there was still an element of danger. Not from the cells but from the chemo we had to have before the transplant.

When my time came, the nurses took me to a private room. Ironically, the room was number seven, the number of completion. It was nice enough and I liked the en-suite facility. However, it's a room I would not wish to return to.

On the first day, I was left to rest and settle in. My vitals were regularly monitored and I was encouraged to eat and to drink plenty of fluids. Later the next day, early in the morning, a nurse arrived with a large jug of ice cubes. I remembered what the nurse on the ward had told me. My heart sank. This was the first of four jugs.

The nurse warned me to eat every single one. She said if I didn't the powerful high dose chemotherapy I was to have before the transplant, would seriously damage my mouth and throat.

She explained that it strips the lining of the gut and stomach and destroys the cancerous cells in the bone marrow. Basically, this chemo destroys everything. There would be no marrow in my bones. I would no longer have any immunity … none at all.

This had to be done, so that my new baby stem cells would be going into a cancer free body. Where they would mature and become healthy bone marrow. I'm probably not explaining it very well. I can't say I fully understand it myself. I just know I felt scared and prayed hard that it would be successful. It was a comfort to know others were praying for me. This transplant was my best and only chance of going into remission.

In the afternoon, after I'd finished four jugs of ice cubes, a nurse arrived with a surprisingly small bag containing the terrifying chemo. I don't know what I expected, a larger bag I suppose, I guess as this chemo is so strong, one didn't need much of it. In no time it was gone and the two head nurses arrived.

The male nurse pushed a container into the room, it resembled a large bomb. He also had some sort of heater. They are both really nice and did their best to encourage me. The male nurse said things like, "Your babies have arrived." This made me smile. Once my temperature and blood pressure were checked, he opened the lid on the bomb, which was the freezer. Taking out a bag he placed it on the heater for a minute or so, and then hung the bag on the hook by my bed and the transfusion began.

I commented on the fact I could smell sweetcorn. They explained it was the solution the stem cells were stored in. The solution either smelt of sweetcorn or tomato sauce. I was glad mine were in sweetcorn, especially as I'm fond of it.

Strangely, as soon as the transfusion began I started to cough and had to keep sipping water. The nurse said it was normal and would pass. I hoped she was right as there were twelve bags still to go. It was early evening by the time it was over.

The nurses who liked the smell of sweetcorn, found any pretext to pop in and see me. Those who didn't like it, stayed away as much as possible, or tried to hold their breath when they came in.

I can't really say when things took a turn for the worse. I suppose it could have been the day after. All I know is, suddenly I felt extremely unwell. For the remainder of that week I lost complete control of my bowel. I don't wish to go into detail, suffice to say I had to wear big nappy things, none of which were totally successful. It was an awful experience … way beyond diarrhoea.

One night during that week, I felt desperately ill. I said to the night nurse, "I want to die."

She replied, "Not on my watch you don't, too much paper work."

I couldn't help smiling. I believe her amusing comment helped me to keep fighting. I liked this nurse and always breathed a sigh of relief when she was on night duty. She was down to earth and amusing. And she was one of the few who made a good cup of tea.

I remained in the hospital in room seven over a week. Then on 30th of August the Doctor told me I could go home. I was delighted, and praised God I had made it through and was fit enough to leave. However, I had lost a lot of weight and had no idea how weak and poorly I was. That is until I tried to stand and pack my few bits to take home. No one helped me. I know the nurses are run off their feet, but I could have done with some help. Anyway, it took a while but I managed it. My driving force was the thought of going home.

Maybe I'm being overly sensitive, but I felt the nurses weren't sorry to see me go. Don't get me wrong, they were never unkind to me and I have no complaints about my treatment. Nevertheless, I found the whole experience traumatic and highly embarrassing. I have never been one to keep ringing the bell to summon a nurse, but there was nothing I could do. I had no control. I felt as though my body had shut down. I feel like crying now, as I write this. And no, I'm not being dramatic. Only those who have had a stem cell transplant will know what I'm saying.

I imagine there are fortunate people whose response to the treatment was different, maybe some people sailed through. But I imagine many will have experienced a similar situation to mine.

I know nurses are used to dealing with sick and sometimes messy patients and for the first time in my life, it was me. For those first few days I was distressed by what was happening to me. There was nothing I could do about it. I have never felt so ill and at one point things could have gone either way.

A few days after I was home, my dear friend Pauline, a lady I used to pray with, told me. God woke her in the middle of the night and told her to pray for me, as I couldn't pray for myself. He told her to clothe me in the armour. She did bless her. I was thrilled when she told me. I was overcome by the awesomeness of God. I still am and always will be.

Keith told me he came to the hospital to see me. It was the day after I'd told the nurse I wanted to die. Before coming into my room, he had asked one of the nurses how I was. She told him I was improving, but she also said, when she got home from work that evening. She told her husband, she felt concerned they could be losing a patient. She was talking about me.

But I thank God for keeping me safe and for the covering of prayer that brought me through. I know without my God and my brothers and sisters, there is every chance I would not be here. Prayer is powerful.

*** ***

Once I'd been told I could go home, I rang Keith and told him. I also suggested that when he arrived at the hospital, he needed to find a wheelchair for me. I knew it wouldn't be easy for him as there is always a shortage, but it's a long walk to the lifts and then a long walk to the car park. I knew, no way would I make it on foot. Bless him. He arrived complete with a wheelchair. I was more than glad to see him. We left the hospital loaded down with medication and my few bits and pieces.

I can't tell you how grateful I was to be home and able to sleep in my own bed. I appreciated the quietness. It's amazing, even at night hospitals are noisy places. I always found it hard to sleep. There's always someone wanting to take your blood pressure or temperature.

That first morning at home was wonderful. I sat up in bed with a cup of tea brought to me by my lovely husband and stared out of the window. It's my favourite thing in the mornings before Keith and I pray together, we like to watch the birds flying around. The Starlings flock together and do amazing aerial acrobatics, especially in the autumn. Sometimes, to our delight a Heron flies by.

Initially, I was weak and thin, but slowly my health and strength returned. Food still tasted horrible, so eating was a bit of a problem. Every weekend, my dear friend Paula brought us a cooked meal. We put one plate in the fridge and shared the other. I'm surprised poor Keith didn't lose weight himself. He spent many weeks sharing his food with me. It was months before I was able to eat a proper meal.

Our church was wonderful. We had no idea they had a few wheelchairs. One was just the right size to fit in our small car. I needed it, as for the next few weeks we had to keep going to the Walsgrave to see the head nurse, to make sure I was doing okay and to have my line cleaned.

It was during one of these visits I had an interesting experience. I remember it clearly. We had seen the head nurse and were making our way to the hospital exit. When Keith decided he needed to use the facilities.

He left me close to the hospital entrance in the wheelchair, where I sat enjoying the warm sunshine. I noticed a tall slim person walk by. It was a lady. There was nothing about the way she was dressed to attract me, her clothing was kind of grey coloured and yet I noticed her. Even with all the people milling around, she stood out.

She stopped and looked at me. She asked me if I was alright. I told her I was waiting for my husband. She smiled and said. "You take care of yourself. You are going to be fine." I was struck by what she said. 'You are going to be fine,' it was said with conviction. I felt encouraged and thanked her.

As she walked away, Keith arrived. I told him about the kind lady and what she had said. I looked for her, but in that short time she had vanished. It was a strange experience and took me by surprise. The memory of it has remained with me, even after all this time. I wondered and still do. Maybe, just maybe she could have been an angel? When I mentioned it to Keith he didn't poo poo it. It was a momentary encounter with a kind stranger. The Bible talks about **entertaining angels unawares**. Hebrews 13 v 2

Eventually, on the 13th of September I saw the head oncologist at the Walsgrave. Her only concern was my weight, she said I was undernourished. I told her I was doing my best to eat. Apart from that she was happy with me and to my delight she released me back into the care of my oncologist at our local hospital.

For the next few weeks I wasn't fit enough to do much. I had managed to find someone to do the garden for us, which was a load off my mind. Poor Keith couldn't do it all.

Thanks to the wheelchair I managed to go to church, but that was about it. When Keith went to play bowls my friend Ruth came and sat with me. On Wednesday mornings I returned to the hospice which I enjoyed. It was nice to sit with others, do some painting or make jewellery.

On the 21st of October I was booked to have

my Hickman line removed. Unfortunately, and much to my annoyance as I was dreading it, it couldn't be done as my silly platelets decided to drop from 49 to 36.

My oncologist was a bit concerned as the line had been in a long time and there was a risk the flesh could have adhered to it. We tried again on the 11th November, I had a blood test and again the platelets were too low. I was getting worried by this time. My oncologist decided to wait a week and then try again. So on the 18th November I had a platelet transfusion followed by the removal of my line. I was scared but relieved.

I didn't need to worry. The Doctor who removed it did loads and was an expert. He was surprised how low it was on my breast. Apparently, most are placed higher up on the chest. I told him where it was had been a bit of a nuisance. He wasn't surprised.

I hung on to the nurse's hand as he gave me a local anaesthetic. What I dreaded had happened. Flesh had adhered to the line. He was going to have to cut me to release it. "It may leave a small scar," he said apologetically.

I shrugged, and told him not to worry about it. At my age did it really matter? He made the incision and after a small tug pulled the line out. I was relieved to see him holding it in his hand.

It had saved me from a lot of cannulas in the back of my hand and had worked wonderfully for my transplant, but boy was I glad to be rid of it. Once he stitched the small cut, I went home. Eight days later I went back to the unit and had the stitches out. He had done a good job. It was just a tiny scar. It was a relief to be free of the line.

With the line out, it was as though the last eighteen months of dare I say hell, was merely a nightmare that had come to an end. Yet strangely, after all the chaos of hospitals and nonstop attention, it felt like an anti-climax. Medically, I felt as though I had been cast adrift. It's all over now. You're on your own.

I was still seeing my oncologist and wasn't in remission as yet, but from my blood tests and from what she said, I was well on the way. She was pleased and so was I. So why was I emotional and tearful? For some reason I was struggling. I said nothing to Keith or any of my friends. The only person who knew how I felt and saw my struggle and tears was God.

God had helped me to find favour with a brilliant Oncologist. I had been given an exceptional treatment plan. Which I found out later cost an awful lot of money. It was a treatment for younger people, not someone of my age. However, the Oncologist felt I was strong enough to cope with it and I had a positive attitude.

She and I liked each other. We did from the first moment we met, when I walked into her office proclaiming, "I don't know why I'm here. There's nothing wrong with me." From that moment, I believe she knew I would be able to cope medically with whatever she threw at me, so to speak.

She didn't know I had someone amazingly powerful looking after me. He strengthened my body and with every situation that occurred, He poured out His peace and covered me with His love.

All through the hellish months of treatment and the stem cell transplant, my faith in Him has grown. I have found a level of spiritual maturity and trust I didn't have before.

Before this nightmare began, I would have said I was a mature Christian, with a strong faith and a deep love of God. All of which is true. But since being afflicted with the beast, which is Mantel Cell Lymphoma, I have found a greater depth of faith and a deeper love for the one who is my Saviour … The Lord Jesus Christ.

Chapter 20

After all the trauma of treatment and hospital visits, Keith and I were blessed to spend a quiet Christmas together. We were supposed to spend Christmas day with our friends, Joy and Bill. Sadly, Bill rang on Christmas Eve to say he had a sore throat. Unfortunately, with my low immunity he felt it would be wise to stay away. I had to agree with him. So Keith and I spent a quiet day together. To be honest, with all that we'd been through it was pleasant to spend some time together at home.

Unfortunately, as is often the case, a few days after Christmas, the 28th to be precise, I rang my GP to see if he could suggest something that would heal an extremely large ulcer I had under my tongue. It was giving me a lot of pain and no matter what I did, it showed no sign of going.

To my surprise he told me to come to the surgery. When I arrived I saw an ambulance parked outside, but didn't think anything of it. I know sooner arrived than he called me into his consulting room, where I learned to my horror, the ambulance was for me. I told him all I had was an ulcer. I didn't need to go to the hospital. He told me my white blood count was extremely low and I had to go.

I continued to argue and protest, finding every obstacle I could think of. I told him my car was parked outside and my husband will wonder where I am. Ignoring my arguments, the Doctor told me the receptionist was ringing my husband and would advise him to come and pick up the car.

I couldn't understand why I had to go to hospital when I felt perfectly well. The Doctor was insistent. He took me to another room where the ambulance staff checked my blood pressure and took my details, before taking me to the ambulance.

Poor Keith, I knew he would be worried. Like me he had assumed I was just seeing the Doctor to get something for the ulcer. As I was whisked off to the Walsgrave, our friend David took Keith to the surgery to pick up the car.

I was not happy. I know the Doctor was trying to help me. I had no idea how poorly I was. But the last place I wanted to go was the hospital, and I was concerned for Keith. I knew he would be worried. As it turned out my white cell count was dangerously low.

Sometime later, I found out I'd had neutropenic sepsis. It was scary and explained why the ulcer wouldn't heal. Realising how close I came to being in big trouble, I was more than grateful for my Doctor's insistence and again thankful for God's wonderful care.

While in the hospital I had my least favourite procedure, a bone barrow biopsy. It wasn't too bad, but they are not nice. I was put on an antibiotic drip, which was continued until a few days before I was discharged.

During my stay in the hospital, I lost a huge amount of weight, which was annoying as I was beginning to put some on, and I suffered with high fevers. Poor Keith came to see me as often as he could. Sometimes he brought my friend Paula which was nice. Ruth and David were also frequent visitors. It was lovely to see them all, I just wished when they went home, I could go with them.

I also had a visit from my oncologist. She had been away and was shocked when she heard I was in the hospital. It was lovely to see her. When she saw me, she sucked in her cheeks to express her shock at my weight loss. I hadn't realised how thin I was.

"What have you been doing?" She asked.

"Nothing," I said with a smile. "All I had was an ulcer under my tongue." But then I became concerned. "Has it come back?" I asked.

She shook her head. "No, it's too soon. Don't worry." She patted my hand and told me when I left the hospital. She would see me in her clinic.

It was lovely to see her and to be reassured. She didn't stay long as Ruth and David were waiting to see me.

It was really funny, a few days later, I saw the Doctor I'd been pestering to let me go home. But my blood count refused to rise, so each time he had to say no. Thank the Lord on Sunday the 8th of January, I saw him go to the nurse's desk and I heard my name mentioned. My blood had been taken earlier, so I guessed they were discussing it. I couldn't hear what he was saying but it sounded positive.

I waited eagerly for him to come and see me. When he appeared he briefly stopped, grinned and pumped the air with his fists. I couldn't help laughing.

"Does that mean I can go home?"

"It does," he said. "We needed your blood count to rise to at least 0.4 and it has. So you can go." He appeared relieved. I'm sure the poor man was glad to see the back of me. I was delighted and couldn't wait to ring Keith and tell him. He was as pleased as me.

He told me that morning in church, one of the ladies had a word from God for me. She said, "The Lord is singing a song over you daily." It really blessed and encouraged me.

I can't tell you how good it was to be home. I was weak and tired, but slowly I gained strength. When I next saw my Oncologist, she was pleased with my progress. Looking at my blood results, she said everything was going in the right direction.

* *
** **

On the 22nd of January, I received some sad news. The husband of my friend Val rang to tell me her stem cell treatment had been unsuccessful and she had passed away in the hospital. The news came as a shock.

Her funeral was on the 24th of January. He knew I couldn't go due to my compromised immunity. However, he wanted to let me know, as he knew during our time together in the hospital, Val and I had become friends. I had given her grandson a signed copy of one of my children's books.

Val's life and mine seemed to run parallel with regard to our treatment. I don't know what cancer Val had, but I know we were both in stage four of rare cancers. She was having her stem cell transplant just after me. However, due to the fact her donor was from Germany, her transplant would be done in a Birmingham hospital. The Walsgrave were I had mine, only catered for patients having their own cells.

She happened to be in the Walsgrave having chemo while I was recuperating after my transplant. Unable to come into the room, she peeked round the door and we had a brief chat. That was the last time I saw her.

She was a lovely lady, always cheerful and fun to be around. One time we happened to be in the hospital together having chemo when Wimbledon was on. She had a laptop and kept us all informed as to who was winning.

I was sad to hear she had died. We were around the same age. Her husband told me she struggled with the transplant and never fully recovered.

There is a risk, even with your own cells. But when you're older and having someone else's cells, that risk is so much higher. Her death saddened me. It also made me realise how blessed and fortunate I am.

Her husband kept in touch for a while. Checking to see how I was and wishing me well. They were a lovely family and both Keith and I had hoped that once Val and I were back on our feet, we would be able to get together. Sadly, it wasn't meant to be.

Cancer is an evil and destructive disease, ruining the lives of young and old alike. It does not discriminate! However, I repeat what I've said before. With Christ Jesus in my life, I am in a win, win situation. I have the greatest physician in my corner and for that I am truly grateful.

* * *

For the next few months' life carried on as normal. I saw my Oncologist regularly and was encouraged by how well I was doing. Each time I saw her, my bloods had improved. On the 7th of June my friend Ruth came with me. I think Keith was out with a friend of his.

The Oncologist was extremely positive. Being as she seemed pleased with me, I asked her if I was in remission, she said, "Yes."

At last it was official. There was no sign of the cancer. Although, she reminds me often, there is no cure and likes to see me every four months, to keep a check on my progress. She's told me if anything happens in between times to get in touch with her. She is so nice. I have her mobile number and am able to contact her should the need arise and there have been times, but I try never to abuse the privilege.

The medical profession may say, for Mantel there is no cure. But I serve a God of miracles. For a woman like me in her early seventies, to have coped and come through such an intense and gruelling procedure is a miracle in itself. I give God all the glory.

Can I say I am cured? No, in all honesty, I can't. What I say next may make you think I am being negative. But believe me, I'm not, I am being realistic. Outside of a miracle from God … which I believe can happen. Mantel Cell Lymphoma does not go away. It returns and each time it does it's worse than the time before.

If God tells me I am cured, believe me I will shout it from the rooftops. To have a miraculous healing from something like Mantel would be awesome. The average length of remission is five years, but some people with a few blips in-between have made it to ten or more years.

As I've said, I'm not a young woman. I could die from any amount of causes not related to Mantel, which would certainly be preferable. However, my life is in God's hands. Whatever is His will is fine by me.

Thanks to Him and the good Doctors He has helped me to find favour with, I am enjoying my life and making the most of every day. I have good and bad days, but then don't we all. There are many who are far worse off than me. So I count myself fortunate and blessed.

I wish I could close this final chapter of my book, by telling you I am cured. But I really can't. To do so would be presumptuous. However, I can tell you this. My life before becoming a Christian was troubled, unhappy and filled with fear and insecurity … not anymore.

On the 3rd of November 1981, the day I met the Lord Jesus, until now in 2019. I have known forgiveness of my sins, acceptance, peace, provision, protection, security, and love beyond measure. Whatever I face in the coming years, I know I will not face it alone. My God has promised, He will never leave me, or forsake me. I am assured of His presence now and into eternity.

This promise is not just for me. It is for all who will accept Jesus Christ as their Saviour and Lord. The words of this beautiful hymn, perfectly express Gods love for us all.

The love of God is greater far, than tongue or pen can ever tell. It goes beyond the highest star and reaches to the lowest hell.

The guilty pair bowed down with care, God gave His son to win. His erring child He reconciled and pardoned from his sin.

Oh love of God, how rich how pure, how measureless and strong. It shall forever more endure the saints and angels song.

Through the pages of this book, I wanted to share how awesome God has been in my life. I hope I have achieved that.

Acknowledgements

The first person I want to thank is the Lord Jesus Christ. Without Him, I could not have coped with the traumatic situations that occurred in my life. His presence was with me through it all.

And a huge thank you to my wonderful husband Keith. I can't tell you how much I appreciate your love and support.

And thank you to my friend Tommie Lyn, for formatting this book for me. I really do appreciate it.

Grateful thanks also, to my dear friend Sue Harrison for the brilliant cover design.

Printed in Poland
by Amazon Fulfillment
Poland Sp. z o.o., Wrocław

61892687R00139